Simply 3 - 5

A collection of recipes using only 3, 4 or 5 ingredients

Fran Winston & Kathy Woods

I

ABOUT SIMPLY 3-5

Simply 3 - 5

About Simply 3-5

Simply 3-5 is not "just another cookery book" that will sit on a shelf, but one you will find really useful over and over again for producing delicious dishes for your family and friends.

ach recipe is easy to follow and requires only a few readily available ingredients. We encourage the use of local, seasonal products wherever possible. The dishes are practical enough for everyday use but also impressive enough to delight your guests when something special is required.

Our recipes include some we grew up with, others we have collected over the years from kitchens around the world, and some we have created especially for you. Many of our recipes have been updated to reflect people's busy lifestyles.

n addition to the helpful tips throughout the book which we hope will encourage you, we also provide a follow up email support service for those of you who have questions, suggestions or ideas.

We believe that Simply 3-5 will become your everyday cookery inspiration and companion, and wish you well on your cookery journey.

SIMPLE THINGS YOU NEED TO KNOW ABOUT 'SIMPLY 3-5'

Simple Things You Need To Know About Simply 3 - 5

Ingredients

- Use local, seasonal products wherever possible as they will be cheaper and of a higher quality. Any other ingredients can be easily found in the supermarket
- Water is not considered an ingredient
- Salt and pepper are not included as ingredients - all savoury recipes should have salt and pepper added to taste
- Oil, butter and margarine are not considered ingredients if being used as the cooking medium, but are considered an ingredient if they are an integral part of the recipe
- Ingredients are listed in the order in which they are added to the recipe
- Crushed garlic in a jar can replace the crushed cloves of garlic - refer to the instructions on the jar you are using for quantity required
- Curry pastes will be different in strength depending on the brand purchased, if you are using an unfamiliar brand and are unsure use a lesser amount and add more if required
- Taste is personal, increase or decrease ingredients such as garlic, herbs, spices and curry pastes to please your own taste

Recipes

- Please read the recipe from beginning to end before you start to cook
- Recipes in each section are in alphabetical order
- Recipes are set out with the ingredient next to the instruction for addition to the recipe
- Vegetarian recipes are marked with a 'V'. There are a number of additional recipes which may be made as vegetarian depending on choice of ingredient, for example, some soups have a choice of chicken or vegetable stock
- Please always check the ingredients listed for any purchased sauces, curry pastes etc to ensure they are vegetarian
- Recipes can be interchanged to suit your needs, for example, lunches can be served as mains (you may need to consider adjusting quantities when interchanging)
- Remember that for many of the recipes the serves can be altered, for example, if the recipe serves 4 and you need it for 8, double it. Equally, you could halve the recipe for 2 serves
- The microwave used in our recipes is 800 watts, adjust cooking times slightly if your microwave wattage differs

Other tips and ideas

- A garnish can enhance the appearance of a dish – consider what you have used in the recipe, for example, sprigs of herbs, finely chopped or julienned vegetables such as red pepper or carrot, a touch of mayonnaise, icings, a dusting of icing sugar, flaked chocolate.
- If you have leftover herbs, chop and freeze in ice cube containers to add to casseroles and soups at a later date
- When cooking if you find you have leftover egg yolks/whites consider adding them to an omelette, scrambled eggs or add water to make an egg wash for glazing pastry. Also, look for a recipe which uses egg yolks or whites only, for example, Carbonara Sauce, Quick and Easy Custard, Mayonnaise, Pavlova, Amaretti Biscuits or Coconut Macaroons
- Cake recipes - insert a skewer into the middle of the cake and if it comes out clean your cake is cooked.

Finally, this book is for you!
Enjoy these recipes with your family and friends....Simply!

CONVERSIONS, MEASURES AND ABBREVIATIONS

Simply 3 - 5

Conversions, Measures and Abbreviations

Spoon Measurements

1.25ml	¼ teaspoon
2.5ml	½ teaspoon
5ml	1 teaspoon
10ml	2 teaspoons
15ml	1 tablespoon

Liquid Cup Measurements

60ml	¼ cup
80ml	⅓ cup
125ml	½ cup
180ml	¾ cup
250ml	1 cup
500ml	2 cups
1 litre	4 cups

Abbreviations

g	grams
kg	kilogram
ml	millilitres
tsp	teaspoon
tbsp	tablespoon
cm	centimetre
cms	centimetres
°C	degrees centigrade
approx	approximately
V	vegetarian

OVEN TEMPERATURES

Simply 3 - 5
Oven Temperatures

You may find oven cooking times will vary a little depending on the oven you are using. Simply 3 - 5 recipe oven temperatures are for fan forced Celsius ovens. As a general rule, for non fan forced ovens, set the oven temperature 10-20°C higher than indicated in the recipe.

	Celsius	Celsius (fan forced)	Fahrenheit	Gas
Very slow	120°C	100°C	250°F	1
Slow	150°C	130°C	300°F	2
Moderately Slow	160°C	140°C	325°F	3
Moderate	180°C	160°C	350°F	4
Moderately Hot	190°C	170°C	375°F	5
Hot	200°C	180°C	400°F	6
Very Hot	230°C	210°C	450°F	7 - 9

CONTENTS

Simply 3 - 5

Contents

Simply 3 - 5

sketches

BREAKFAST

Simply 3 - 5

Breakfast

AVOCADO AND LIME WITH BACON ON TOAST

Simply 3 - 5

Avocado and Lime with Bacon on Toast

Serves 4

2 ripe avocados
2 tbsp lime juice

Halve, deseed and peel avocados. Slice lengthways into 1cm slices and place in a large bowl. Drizzle with the lime juice and toss gently. Set aside for 10 minutes.

175g back bacon rashers, chopped

Meanwhile, fry the bacon over a medium heat until golden and crisp.

8 thick slices bread
butter, for spreading

Toast the bread for 1-2 minutes each side until golden. Spread lightly with the butter.

Place toast on plates, top with the bacon and avocado.

BACON AND ONION OMELETTE

Bacon and Onion Omelette

Serves 2

1 tbsp olive oil
½ small onion, finely chopped
2 rashers back bacon, chopped

4 eggs

Heat the oil and gently fry the onion and bacon together until the onion is soft and bacon is cooked through.

Meanwhile, beat the eggs until well mixed. Pour the eggs evenly over the top of the bacon and onion mixture. Cook on a low heat until the egg is cooked through. Gently fold in half and serve.

BIRCHER MUESLI

Bircher Muesli v

Serves 4

250g muesli
350ml milk
125ml single cream
130g Greek style yoghurt

2 apples, coarsely grated
extra Greek style yoghurt, to serve

Place the muesli in a bowl or airtight container and add the milk, cream and yoghurt. Mix until well combined. Cover and place in the fridge overnight.

When ready to serve stir in most of the grated apple reserving a little. Divide the muesli among the serving dishes and top with extra yoghurt and reserved apple.

Note: Needs to be served immediately or apple will go brown.

BREAKFAST IN A GLASS

Simply 3 - 5

Breakfast in a Glass v

Serves 1

100ml strawberry yoghurt
1 weetabix, crushed
1 banana, chopped
250ml pineapple juice

Place all ingredients in a blender or food processor and process until smooth and creamy.
Pour into a glass.

Note: You can use any flavoured yoghurt.

Simply 2

CREAM CHEESE AND CHIVE CROISSANT

Cream Cheese and Chive Croissant v

Serves 6

6 croissants

250g cream cheese,
at room temperature
1 tsp Dijon mustard
1 tsp grated lemon rind
1 tbsp lemon juice
2 tbsp chopped chives

Preheat oven to 180°C.

Heat the croissants in the oven for a few minutes.

Meanwhile, beat the cheese, mustard, lemon rind and lemon juice until soft and creamy. Stir in the chives.

Split the croissants and spread with the cheese and chive mixture.

CREAMY MARMALADE TOASTED SANDWICHES

Creamy Marmalade Toasted Sandwiches v

Makes 4 sandwiches

125g cream cheese,
at room temperature
50g dried apricots, finely chopped
1 tsp finely grated orange rind

8 slices of raisin bread
4 tbsp marmalade

Place the cream cheese in a bowl and beat until light and creamy. Add the apricots and orange rind and mix with a spoon until combined.

Spread the mixture over four slices of the raisin bread. Spread the remaining slices of raisin bread with the marmalade. Sandwich a cream cheese slice and a marmalade slice together.

Add a little olive oil to a frying pan and heat over a medium heat. Add one or two of the sandwiches and cook on both sides until golden and warmed through.

Repeat to cook the remaining sandwiches, adding a little more oil if required.

CREAMY PORRIDGE WITH STEWED RHUBARB

Creamy Porridge with Stewed Rhubarb v

Serves 4

500g rhubarb, trimmed and cut into 3cm lengths
75g caster sugar

Place the rhubarb and sugar in a saucepan and stir over a low heat until the sugar dissolves. Increase heat until gently simmering. Cook, uncovered, stirring occasionally, for 15 minutes or until rhubarb is just tender.

180g porridge oats
750ml milk
250ml single cream

Meanwhile, combine oats, milk and cream in a saucepan and cook over a low heat, stirring often, until thick and creamy and the oats are tender. Add more milk if necessary to achieve desired consistency.

Spoon porridge into serving bowls and top with rhubarb.

EGGS BENEDICT WITH CHORIZO

Eggs Benedict with Chorizo

Serves 4

4 eggs

Poach the eggs and spoon onto kitchen paper.

1 tbsp oil
16 slices chorizo sausage
4 English muffins, cut in half and toasted

Heat the oil, fry the chorizo until golden then divide between 4 muffin halves.

8 tbsp hollandaise sauce

Place poached eggs on the chorizo and smother with hollandaise. Top with other half of muffin.

Note: Use store bought hollandaise sauce as there are some very good ones available. For a traditional Eggs Benedict replace the chorizo with 2 grilled slices of streaky bacon for each person.

HEARTY ALL IN ONE BREAKFAST

Hearty All in One Breakfast

Serves 4

4 sausages
4 large portobello mushrooms
2 tbsp olive oil

4 back bacon rashers
4 small ripe plum tomatoes,
halved lengthways

4 eggs

Preheat oven to 180°C.

Arrange the sausages and mushrooms in a large roasting tin. Drizzle the oil over and bake in the oven for 10 minutes, turning once.

Add the bacon and tomatoes and bake for a further 7 minutes or until mushrooms and tomato are soft. Arrange the mixture in the tin creating 4 spaces.

Crack one egg into each space and bake for 4-5 minutes or until the eggs are cooked to your liking. Turn eggs once if preferred.

Note: You can use oiled egg rings if you like.

MINI BACON AND SPINACH FRITTATAS

Mini Bacon and Spinach Frittatas

Makes 12

1 tbsp olive oil
6 rashers back bacon, chopped
100g baby spinach, chopped

8 eggs
180ml milk
100g mature cheese, grated

Preheat oven to 180°C.

Heat oil in a frying pan and fry bacon until just cooked, add spinach and cook for 1 minute. Divide equally between a 12 hole muffin tray.

Combine eggs with milk and cheese. Pour into the muffin tins and bake for 20 minutes.

Note: These can be eaten hot or cold. They are also great for a picnic.

SCRAMBLED EGGS WITH SPINACH AND FETA

Scrambled Eggs with Spinach and Feta v

Serves 2

3 eggs
2 tbsp milk

1 tbsp olive oil

50g feta cheese, crumbled
25g baby spinach leaves

Mix the eggs and milk together in a bowl.

Heat oil in a frying pan then pour in the egg mixture and cook gently, stirring, for 2 minutes.

Add the feta cheese and spinach to the mixture and continue to cook to your liking.

SMOKED SALMON AND DILL OMELETTE

Smoked Salmon and Dill Omelette

Serves 1

3 eggs
3 tbsp milk

Using a fork whisk the eggs and milk together.

20g butter

Melt the butter in a 20cm frying pan and pour in the egg mixture. Move the egg mixture around for 30 seconds.

40g smoked salmon, chopped
1 tbsp chopped dill

Scatter the salmon and dill over the top of the eggs. When the eggs are cooked to your liking, fold over and serve.

DIPS, NIBBLES AND STARTERS

Simply 3 - 5

Dips, Nibbles and Starters

Dips

Nibbles and Starters

DIPS, NIBBLES AND STARTERS

Simply 3 - 5

Dips, Nibbles and Starters

Nibbles and Starters

CLASSIC FRENCH ONION DIP

CREAMY THAI DIP

HORSERADISH, BEETROOT AND CRÈME FRAICHE DIP

Simply 3 - 5

Classic French Onion Dip v

250g cream cheese
⅓ of a packet of
French onion soup mix
4 tbsp milk

Using a fork blend all ingredients together in a bowl.

Note: We use a packet of Knorr French onion soup (dried).

Add the soup to taste because if you add too much it will be salty. If you like a thinner consistency just add a little more milk.

Creamy Thai Dip v

150g low fat natural yoghurt
5 tbsp mayonnaise
2 spring onions, finely sliced

2 tbsp sweet chilli sauce

Mix yoghurt, mayonnaise and spring onions together.

Stir chilli sauce into dip.

Horseradish, Beetroot and Crème Fraiche Dip v

2 tbsp hot horseradish sauce
250g cooked beetroot
(not in vinegar), roughly chopped
100ml crème fraiche

Place all the ingredients in a food processor or blender and process until smooth.

Note: This is a really beautiful colour.

RED PEPPER HOUMOUS

SMOKED SALMON AND HORSERADISH DIP

BAKED CAMEMBERT

Simply 3 - 5

Red Pepper Houmous v

1 red pepper
1 tbsp olive oil

Cut pepper into strips and fry gently in the oil until tender.

400g can chickpeas, drained and rinsed
2 cloves garlic, peeled
lemon juice, to taste

Process the chickpeas, red pepper, garlic and 2 teaspoons lemon juice in a food processor or blender. Taste, and add more lemon juice, if necessary.

Smoked Salmon and Horseradish Dip

60g smoked salmon
200g cream cheese
100ml yoghurt
2 tbsp horseradish cream
1 tbsp lemon juice

Place all ingredients in a food processor and process until smooth.

Baked Camembert v

Serves 2

Preheat oven to 180°C.

1 Camembert, in a box
a few thyme leaves
1 tbsp olive oil

Unwrap the cheese and carefully slice the rind off the top of the cheese. Return the cheese to the box, cut side up. Sprinkle with the thyme and drizzle over the oil. Place the cheese in its box on a baking sheet.

Bake for 10-15 minutes until the cheese has melted.
Serve immediately.

Note: We sometimes sprinkle some finely sliced spring onions onto this instead of the thyme.

CHEESE AND HERB PATE

FIGS AND BAKED RICOTTA CHEESE

Simply 3 - 5

Cheese and Herb Pate v

Serves 8 as a starter

150g butter

Melt the butter and allow to cool.

450g cream cheese
3 cloves garlic, crushed
1 tbsp finely chopped
flat leaf parsley
2 tbsp finely chopped chives

Mix cheese, garlic, parsley and chives together. Fold the melted butter into the cream cheese mixture. Fold it in very carefully or it could curdle. Transfer the mixture to a loaf tin or suitable serving dish and put in fridge for a few hours to chill.

Note: This is lovely served as a starter with salad leaves and melba toast. Alternatively, it can be served as a lunch with a salad and bread.

Figs and Baked Ricotta Cheese v

Serves 6

Preheat oven to 180°C.

500g ricotta cheese
a little fresh thyme and rosemary
leaves
1 tbsp extra virgin olive oil

Place ricotta in a baking dish and scatter with thyme and rosemary. Drizzle with the oil and bake for 15 minutes.

6 ripe figs, halved

Add the figs and bake for a further 10 minutes.

FRESH GOAT'S CHEESE WITH RASPBERRY COULIS

HALLOUMI WITH CHILLI OIL AND LIME

Simply 3 - 5

Fresh Goat's Cheese with Raspberry Coulis v

Serves 4

2 goat's cheese logs

Chill goat's cheese well then cut each log into 10 rounds.

225g fresh raspberries
25-30g caster sugar

Crush the raspberries with a fork and press through a fine sieve to extract the juice. Add sugar to taste, but make sure the coulis stays sharp tasting.

salad leaves, to serve
8 mint leaves, finely sliced

Divide the salad leaves between the plates and place 5 rounds of cheese on top. Drizzle with the raspberry coulis and sprinkle with mint.

Note: We use La Buche goat's cheese logs but any creamy goat's cheese will work. This is so simple but so delicious.

Halloumi with Chilli Oil and Lime v

Serves 6

1 tbsp olive oil
2 x 250g packs halloumi, sliced

Heat the oil in a frying pan on medium heat and cook the halloumi in batches for a few minutes on each side until golden.

2 bags mixed leaf salad
6 tbsp chilli oil
½ tsp chilli flakes

Arrange salad leaves on 6 plates and top with a few halloumi slices. Drizzle with the chilli oil and sprinkle with a few chilli flakes.

lime wedges, to serve

Squeeze a little lime juice over the top.

39

MEDITERRANEAN TRIANGLES

MUSHROOM AND BACON SKEWERS

Simply 3 - 5
Mediterranean Triangles v

Makes 18

Preheat oven to 180°C.

50g pine nuts
250g ricotta cheese
75g finely chopped
semidried tomatoes
2 tbsp basil pesto

Gently toast the pine nuts in a
frying pan. Combine the ricotta,
pine nuts, tomatoes and pesto
and mix well.

6 sheets filo pastry

Lay one sheet of filo pastry
lengthways and brush lightly with
olive oil. Place a second sheet on
top and cut the pastry lengthways
into 6 even strips.

Place 2 teaspoons of the
combined mixture on the bottom
left hand corner of one strip and
fold over to form a triangle.
Continue with remaining pastry
and mixture.

olive oil, for brushing

Brush the tops lightly with olive
oil and bake in the oven for
10-15 minutes.

Mushroom and Bacon Skewers

Makes 8

You will need 8 bamboo skewers
for this recipe (See note).

400g button mushrooms

Place mushrooms in a shallow
dish in a single layer.

150ml reduced salt soy sauce
2 tbsp sweet chilli sauce
2 tbsp olive oil

Combine soy sauce, chilli
sauce and oil and pour over
mushrooms. Toss to coat,
cover and set aside for 30 mins.

8 rashers back bacon,
rind removed

Thread mushrooms and bacon
onto skewer. Thread the bacon
in a concertina fashion. Heat a
frying pan over a medium high
heat and cook the skewers,
turning often, for 10 minutes.

Note: Soak the skewers in cold
water for 30 minutes prior to
using to prevent them from
burning.

OLIVE PESTO PUFFS

PEACHES WRAPPED IN PROSCIUTTO

Simply 3 - 5

Olive Pesto Puffs v

Makes 20

Preheat oven to 200°C.

1 sheet frozen puff pastry, thawed

Using a 5cm round cutter, cut out rounds from the pastry sheet. Place the rounds on oven trays lined with baking paper.

3 tbsp sundried tomato paste
10 black olives, pitted and halved lengthways
50g crumbled feta cheese
20g finely grated Parmesan cheese

Spread tomato paste evenly over each round. Top each with an olive half then sprinkle with a little feta cheese then a little Parmesan cheese.

Cook for 10 minutes or until the pastry and cheese are golden.

Peaches wrapped in Prosciutto

Serves 4

2 peaches
6 slices prosciutto, halved
80g bag rocket or mixed salad leaves

Cut each peach into six wedges and wrap each wedge in a prosciutto half. Place on serving plates with the salad.

125ml balsamic vinegar
50g brown sugar

Place the vinegar and sugar into a frying pan over high heat and boil until thickened. Cool slightly, spoon over the peaches, and serve.

PIEDMONTESE PEPPERS

ROASTED AUBERGINE, TOMATO AND FETA

Simply 3 - 5

Piedmontese Peppers v

Serves 4

4 thin slices onion
4 small tomatoes,
cut in half and deseeded
2 red peppers, cut in half and
deseeded
1 tbsp dried thyme
2 tbsp olive oil

Preheat oven to 180°C.
Place 1 onion slice and 2
tomato halves in each pepper
half, sprinkle with the thyme
and then drizzle the oil over.

Bake in the oven for about 20
minutes, or until the peppers
are tender but not collapsed.

Roasted Aubergine, Tomato and Feta v

Serves 4

1 large aubergine cut into 8 rounds,
1cm thick

2 large tomatoes, sliced into
8 rounds
a few basil leaves, shredded
250g feta cheese, cut into 8 slices
olive oil, for drizzling

Preheat oven to 180°C.
Fry the aubergine in a little oil
until slightly softened.

Place the aubergine on a baking
tray. Top each slice of aubergine
with a slice of tomato, a
sprinkle of basil and a slice of
feta. Drizzle with olive oil and
bake for about 20 minutes.

SALMON AND CUCUMBER WITH DILL MAYONNAISE

SPICY PITTA CRISPS

Simply 3 - 5

Salmon and Cucumber with Dill Mayonnaise

Makes 18

125ml mayonnaise 2 tbsp lemon juice 3 tsp finely chopped dill, plus extra sprigs to garnish	Combine the mayonnaise, lemon juice and chopped dill.
½ cucumber, approx 100g smoked salmon	Cut the cucumber into 18 x 1cm slices. Cut the salmon into 18 strips. Folding as necessary, place a piece of salmon on top of each cucumber slice. Top with a little mayonnaise and garnish with a sprig of dill.

Spicy Pitta Crisps v

Makes 40

	Preheat oven to 180°C.
5 large pitta breads	Split each pitta bread in half, cut each half into quarters. Place in a single layer on oven trays.
4 tbsp olive oil 1 tsp Cajun seasoning	Brush with oil and sprinkle with seasoning. Bake for about 10 minutes or until brown and crispy.

Note: These are great served with dips.

SPINACH AND BLUE CHEESE TARTLET

Simply 3 - 5

Spinach and Blue Cheese Tartlet v

Serves 4

Preheat oven to 180°C.

125g baby leaf spinach

Put the spinach in a saucepan with 2 tablespoons of water and cook for approximately 3 minutes. Drain well.

200g shortcrust pastry

Divide the pastry into 4 equal pieces. Roll out to line 4 x 10cm tartlet tins. Bake blind for about 15 minutes.
Remove from oven and lower oven temperature to 140°C

125g Stilton or Danish blue cheese

Cut the cheese into 1cm cubes.

2 eggs
4 tbsp milk

Mix together eggs and milk then half fill each of the tartlet tins.

Push the spinach into the egg mixture leaving gaps for the cheese to be put in. Place cheese in the gaps.

Bake for about 15 minutes or until the egg is set.

Note: The tartlets are best served warm/hot so the cheese remains melted.

Other cheeses such as Brie and Gorgonzola also work well.

STIR FRIED GARLIC PRAWNS

TAPENADE TWISTS

Simply 3 - 5

Stir Fried Garlic Prawns

Serves 4

1 tbsp olive oil
3 cloves garlic, crushed
1 fresh red chilli, seeded and
finely chopped

600g large raw peeled prawns
1 tbsp chopped flat leaf parsley

Heat the oil in a large frying
pan. Add the garlic and chilli
and stir fry until fragrant but not
coloured.

Add the prawns and stir fry until
the prawns have just changed
in colour. Serve sprinkled with
parsley.

Tapenade Twists

Makes approx 32

Preheat oven to 200°C.

4 tbsp black olive tapenade
2 sheets frozen puff pastry, thawed
4 tbsp finely grated Parmesan
cheese

Spread the tapenade equally
across both sheets of pastry.
Sprinkle evenly with the
Parmesan and fold each sheet
in half pressing firmly to seal.

Cut the pastry into 1.5cm strips.
Take both ends of each pastry
strip and twist in opposite
directions.

Place on a baking sheet lined
with baking paper and bake for
7 minutes or until golden.

SOUP

Simply 3 - 5

Soup

CARROT AND COURGETTE SOUP

Carrot and Courgette Soup

Serves 4

25g butter
300g carrots, peeled and chopped
250g courgettes, chopped

600ml vegetable or chicken stock
1 tsp sugar
1 tbsp tomato puree

Melt the butter in a saucepan and gently fry the vegetables for 10 minutes without colouring.

Add stock, sugar and tomato puree.

Simmer for 30 minutes then process or blend until smooth.

CHICKEN AND CORN SOUP

Simply 3 - 5

Chicken and Corn Soup

Serves 4

300g cooked chicken, shredded
1 x 418g can creamed corn
750ml chicken stock

Place all ingredients in a saucepan, bring to the boil then simmer for 5 minutes.

Note: Leftover roast chicken is ideal for use in this soup.

Medicinal Mushroom Soup

CREAM OF MUSHROOM SOUP

Cream of Mushroom Soup

Serves 4

1 tbsp olive oil 1 small onion, finely chopped	Heat oil in a saucepan, add onion and gently fry until soft but not coloured.
500g mushrooms, chopped 1.5 litres vegetable or chicken stock	Add the mushrooms and stock then cook, covered, for 10 minutes.
125ml double cream	Stir in the cream. Process or blend the soup and gently reheat.

CREAM OF ONION SOUP

Simply 3 - 5

Cream of Onion Soup v

Serves 4

50g butter plus 25g extra
1kg onions, chopped

Melt the 60g butter in a large saucepan. Keep 200g of the onions aside and add the rest to the pan. Stir, cover and cook very gently without colouring for about 30 minutes.

Meanwhile, melt the extra 25g of butter in another pan and cook remaining onions over a low heat, covered, until soft, but not coloured. Uncover and cook until they turn pale golden brown. Set aside and add with cream at the end.

1 litre vegetable stock

After 30 minutes add stock, bring to boil then simmer for a further 5 minutes.
Process or blend until smooth.

150ml double cream

Add cream and onions to the soup and reheat gently.

Note: If you want a completely smooth soup just cook all the onions together at the start. This is delicious and has a mild flavour.

CREAM OF ROASTED TOMATO SOUP

Simply 3 - 5

Cream of Roasted Tomato Soup v

Serves 4

2kg tomatoes, halved

2 tbsp olive oil
2 cloves garlic, crushed
1 tbsp balsamic vinegar

100ml double cream

Preheat oven to 160°C.

Place tomatoes, cut side down, on roasting tray.

Mix oil, garlic and vinegar together and pour over the tomatoes. Cook in the oven for 50 minutes or until soft. Remove from oven and when cool enough to handle remove the skins. Process or blend until smooth.

Reheat gently then add cream.

Note: If the tomatoes are soft enough you will be able to remove the skins easily.

LEEK AND POTATO SOUP

Leek and Potato Soup v

Serves 4

25g butter
400g leeks, washed and sliced

Melt butter in a saucepan add leeks, cover and cook without colouring until soft.

750ml vegetable stock
2 bouquet garni
200g peeled potatoes, diced

Add the stock, bouquet garni and potatoes. Simmer, for about 15 minutes or until potatoes are tender. Remove bouquet garni.

Note: This soup can be served with the vegetables whole or processed until smooth.
You can also fry some thinly sliced leeks until they are crispy to use as a garnish.

PUMPKIN AND GINGER SOUP

Pumpkin and Ginger Soup

Serves 8

2 tbsp olive oil
1 onion, chopped
2kg pumpkin,
peeled and chopped
4cm fresh ginger,
peeled and chopped

2 tbsp soy sauce
875ml vegetable or chicken stock

Heat the oil in a saucepan and add the onion, pumpkin and ginger. Gently fry without colouring until the vegetables are soft. Process or blend the vegetables until smooth.

Add the soy sauce and stock. Reheat gently and serve.

Note: You can scrape the ginger skin off with a teaspoon which is much easier than any other way.

STILTON AND WATERCRESS SOUP

Simply 3 - 5

Stilton and Watercress Soup

Serves 4

600ml vegetable or chicken stock
225g watercress,
large stalks removed

Put the stock in a saucepan and
bring to the boil. Add the
watercress and simmer for
about 3 minutes until tender.

150g Stilton cheese, crumbled
150ml double cream

Add the cheese and simmer for
a further minute until the cheese
has started to melt. Process or
blend the soup until smooth then
stir in the cream.

Reheat gently and serve.

Note: This soup is good for a
dinner party.

Tomato and Lentil Soup

TOMATO AND LENTIL SOUP

Simply 3 - 5

Tomato and Lentil Soup v

Serves 4

1 tbsp olive oil
1 large onion, finely chopped

2 tbsp mild curry paste
2 x 400g cans chopped tomatoes
1 litre vegetable stock
200g red lentils

Heat oil in a saucepan and
gently fry the onion until soft
and golden.

Stir in the curry paste then
add the rest of the ingredients.
Bring to the boil and simmer,
stirring occasionally, over a
low heat for about 20 minutes
or until the lentils are soft.

Note: This is a thick and hearty
soup. Add more stock or water
if a thinner consistency is
preferred.

TUSCAN BEAN SOUP

Tuscan Bean Soup

Serves 4

2 tbsp olive oil
1 onion, chopped
2 cloves garlic, crushed
3-4 sprigs fresh thyme

Heat the oil in a saucepan and gently fry the onion, garlic and thyme for 3-4 minutes.

4 x 400g cans cannellini beans
1 litre vegetable or chicken stock

Drain the beans and rinse well with cold water. Add the beans and stock to the saucepan and cook over a medium heat for about 5 minutes. Process or blend the soup so it retains some texture.

LUNCH

Simply 3 - 5

Lunch

LUNCH

Simply 3 - 5

Lunch

AUBERGINE AND TOMATO PARMIGIANA

Aubergine and Tomato Parmigiana v

Serves 6

Preheat oven to 180°C.
Lightly grease a 6cm deep,
22 x 22cm square ovenproof
dish.

4 large aubergines, thinly sliced
200ml olive oil, for brushing

Brush aubergine slices with oil
and cook in a frying pan for 2-3
minutes each side. Transfer to
a plate and repeat with the
remaining aubergine and oil.

700g passata
1 bunch basil, leaves torn
500g mozzarella cheese, grated
120g Parmesan cheese,
finely grated

Layer a quarter of the eggplant
over the base of the dish. Spoon
over a third of the passata and
a third of the basil. Sprinkle
over a quarter of the mozzarella
cheese. Repeat layers twice.

Top with remaining aubergine.
Combine remaining mozzarella
cheese with the Parmesan and
sprinkle over the aubergine.

Bake for 30 minutes or until
golden.

BEEF ROLLS

Beef Rolls

Makes 12 small rolls

Preheat oven to 200°C.

Line 2 baking sheets with baking paper.

500g lean minced beef
4 tbsp tomato ketchup
1 onion, finely chopped
2 tbsp fresh flat leaf parsley, chopped

Combine beef, ketchup, onion and parsley in a large mixing bowl and divide into four portions.

2 sheets frozen puff pastry, thawed

Cut each sheet of pastry in half. Lay one portion of mince mixture along the long side of the pastry to form a sausage shape. Roll pastry over mince to enclose.

Place seam side down and cut into 3 pieces. Place on the baking sheets and repeat with remaining pastry and mince mixture.

Bake for 20-25 minutes until puffed, golden and cooked through.

BLUE CHEESE VEGETABLE GRATIN

Blue Cheese Vegetable Gratin v

Serves 4-6

450g potatoes, thickly sliced
450g carrots, thickly sliced
450g parsnips, thickly sliced

30g butter
1 bunch spring onions, roughly chopped

200g Stilton cheese

Preheat oven to 180°C.

Place potatoes, carrots and parsnips in a large saucepan, cover with cold water and bring to the boil. Lower heat and simmer for about 10 minutes until just tender. Drain well, and set aside.

Melt the butter in the pan you cooked the vegetables in, add the spring onions and fry gently for a minute or two until slightly softened.

Add the vegetables to the pan and stir gently until coated with butter. Tip into a buttered shallow ovenproof dish. Slice the cheese and arrange over the top of the vegetables. Bake for 20 minutes or until the cheese has melted. Serve hot.

Note: This is good as a light lunch or served with grilled chicken or cold meats as a more substantial meal.

BRIE AND TOMATO TART

Simply 3 - 5

Brie and Tomato Tart v

Serves 4

250g puff pastry

225g courgettes
2 tbsp olive oil

225g Brie
4-5 large tomatoes

Preheat oven to 190°C.

Roll out the pastry to a 23 x 30cm oblong and place on a baking sheet. Use a knife to score the pastry 2.5cm from the edge on all 4 sides. Prick the base with a fork, inside the scoring.

Slice the courgettes into thin slices. Heat the oil in a frying pan and fry the courgettes for 1-2 minutes until softened then cool slightly.

While the courgettes are cooling slice the Brie and tomatoes into thin slices.

Starting from the short end of the pastry, arrange, within the scoring marks four overlapping rows of Brie, tomatoes and courgettes. Bake for 25-30 minutes until the pastry is puffed up and the courgettes are tender. Serve warm.

Note: This looks really good and tastes delicious.

CHICKEN, AVOCADO AND CHEESE MELTS

Chicken, Avocado and Cheese Melts

Serves 4

4 large slices of ciabatta

Place the bread on a tray under the grill and lightly toast.

500g chicken breast, cooked and shredded
2 avocados, sliced
200g semidried tomatoes, chopped
8 slices Jarlsberg cheese

Remove from the grill and top with the chicken, avocado, tomatoes and cheese. Return to the grill and cook for a few minutes until the cheese melts.

CHORIZO, GRUYERE AND OLIVE FRITTATA

Chorizo, Gruyere and Olive Frittata

Serves 4

Preheat oven to 180°C.

Lightly grease a deep 20cm round cake tin. Line base and sides with baking paper.

6 eggs
125ml double cream

Whisk eggs and cream together in bowl.

150g chorizo slices
100g Gruyere cheese, grated
100g pitted green olives, chopped

Cook chorizo in a frying pan, stirring, for about 5 minutes or until crisp then drain on kitchen paper. Layer half the cheese, olives and chorizo in a dish. Pour over half the egg mixture then repeat the layering.

Cook, uncovered, for about 30 minutes or until the frittata is set. Stand for 10 minutes before cutting.

GARLIC, POTATO AND CHEESE PIZZA

Garlic, Potato and Cheese Pizza v

Serves 2

2 cloves garlic, crushed
3 tbsp olive oil
1 x 25cm pizza base

2 medium potatoes, peeled
and very thinly sliced
100g mozzarella cheese

Preheat oven to 200°C.

Combine the garlic with 2 tablespoons of the olive oil and brush over the pizza base.

Arrange the potato slices over the base ensuring you take them right out to the edges. Brush the potato with the last tablespoon of oil. Top with the mozzarella cheese and bake for 15 minutes or until the potatoes are tender.

GREEK SALAD
TORTILLAS

Simply 3 - 5

Greek Salad Tortillas v

Serves 2

2 large soft tortilla wraps

Warm a pan over a medium heat then quickly toss the tortillas in one at a time just to warm them through slightly.

2 heaped tbsp houmous

Spread the houmous over the tortillas.

1 large ripe tomato, roughly chopped
5cm piece of cucumber, cut into sticks
60g feta cheese, cubed

Make a row of tomato, cucumber and feta down the centre of each tortilla.

Fold the sides to seal in the ingredients and roll up tightly. Cut each tortilla in half and serve.

JACKET POTATOES WITH FLAVOURED BUTTERS

Jacket Potatoes with Flavoured Butters v

Serves 4

Preheat oven to 190°C

4 baking potatoes, scrubbed and pricked with a fork

Bake potatoes in oven for 50-60 minutes until crisp on the outside and tender inside. When cooked, top with a slice of your chosen flavoured butter.

Spicy red pepper butter

1 roasted red pepper, from jar
125g unsalted butter, softened
2 drops Tabasco sauce

Finely chop the red pepper and mix butter, pepper and Tabasco together well.

Cheese, chive and tomato butter

125g unsalted butter, softened
75g mature cheese, finely grated
2 tbsp snipped chives
1 tbsp tomato puree

Mix all ingredients together.

Herb and garlic butter

125g unsalted butter, softened
4 tbsp of chopped parsley, chives or dill
1 clove garlic, crushed

Mix all ingredients together.

Note: Spoon the butters onto clingfilm, roll up into sausage shapes and chill. These butters will keep for about 2 weeks in the fridge. They are also great served over grilled chicken or steak.

LEMON AND GARLIC CHICKEN DRUMSTICKS

Simply 3 - 5

Lemon and Garlic Chicken Drumsticks

Serves 4

3 cloves garlic, crushed
80ml olive oil
1 lemon, juice and
finely grated rind

8 chicken drumsticks

Combine the garlic, oil, lemon rind and juice in a large bowl.

Carefully make a few slashes in the skin of the drumsticks. Add the drumsticks to the marinade and toss to coat evenly. Cover and refrigerate for at least one hour.

Preheat oven to 190°C. Drain the chicken and discard the marinade. Place the drumsticks in a roasting tin and cook for approximately 25 minutes or until crispy and cooked through.

Note: This also works well with chicken wings, thighs or breast fillets, but you may need to adjust cooking times.

LENTIL
BURGERS

Lentil Burgers v

Serves 2-4

200g red lentils
500ml water

Wash the lentils and place in a saucepan with the water. Bring to the boil then simmer very gently for 15 minutes or until all the water has been absorbed.

1 tsp curry paste
2 tbsp spring vegetable dried soup mix
2 tbsp chopped flat leaf parsley
1 tbsp flour

Add curry paste, soup mix and parsley to the lentils, mix to combine. Refrigerate for 30 minutes. Divide mix into 4 and shape to form burgers, dust with the flour.

1-2 tbsp oil, for frying

Heat the oil in a non stick frying pan, add the burgers and cook for 4-5 minutes on each side until golden brown.

Note: These can be served with chutney and a salad or in a burger bun with salad.

MOZZARELLA, HAM AND PESTO PIZZAS

Mozzarella, Ham and Pesto Pizzas

Serves 2

Preheat grill to high.

4 mini pitta breads

Put the pittas on the grill rack and heat for about 1 minute.

4 tsp basil pesto
50-60g smoked, wafer thin ham
150g pack mozzarella, sliced into 4 slices

Turn the pittas over and spread each one with 1 teaspoon of pesto then top with ham and a mozzarella slice.

Return to the grill for 3-4 minutes until cheese has melted and started to turn golden.

OVEN BAKED PARMESAN RISOTTO

Oven Baked Parmesan Risotto

Serves 4-6

300g risotto rice
1 litre chicken stock

75g Parmesan cheese,
finely grated
40g butter

Preheat oven to 180°C.

Place the rice and stock in a large baking dish and stir to combine. Cover tightly with foil or a lid and bake for 45 minutes or until most of the stock is absorbed and the rice is just cooked.

Add the Parmesan and butter and stir for 3-4 minutes or until the risotto is thick and creamy.

PURPLE SPROUTING BROCCOLI WITH HAM AND CHEESE

Purple Sprouting Broccoli with Ham and Cheese

Serves 2 for lunch or 4 as a snack

400g purple sprouting broccoli

Bring a pan of water to the boil, add the broccoli and simmer for 2 minutes. Drain into a colander and cool under running cold water.

200g carton crème fraiche
1 tbsp wholegrain mustard
100g grated cheese, Gruyere or Cheddar

In a bowl mix the crème fraiche with the mustard and half the cheese.
Preheat the grill to high.

8 slices ham

Use each slice of ham to wrap up 3 or 4 stems of broccoli then place in a baking dish. Spread the creamy mixture over the ham and broccoli and sprinkle with the remaining cheese. Grill for 7-10 minutes or until golden and bubbly.

Note: If you can't get purple sprouting broccoli just use tender stem broccoli.

RED PEPPER AND BACON CAULIFLOWER CHEESE

Red Pepper and Bacon Cauliflower Cheese

Serves 4

1 cauliflower, broken into florets

Cook the cauliflower in a pan of boiling water for about 6-7 minutes until just tender. Drain, then place in a shallow ovenproof dish.

Preheat grill to high.

6 rashers back bacon
230g jar roasted red peppers, drained and cut into strips

Grill the bacon until crisp then cut into large pieces. Add half the bacon to the cauliflower, along with the red peppers and stir lightly.

200ml crème fraiche
175g mature Cheddar, grated

Mix together the crème fraiche and all but a handful of cheese. Spread mixture over the vegetables then sprinkle over the remaining bacon and cheese. Grill for about 5 minutes or until the top is bubbling and golden.

Note: This is really good. Leave the bacon out if serving vegetarians.

ROAST PUMPKIN AND FETA PIES

Roast Pumpkin and Feta Pies v

Makes 10

Preheat oven to 190°C.

400g pumpkin, peeled and cut
into 1cm pieces
2 tsp olive oil

Place pumpkin onto a baking
sheet lined with baking paper,
drizzle with oil and bake for 20
minutes or until tender.

2 sheets frozen puff pastry, thawed

Lightly grease 10 holes in a
muffin pan. Cut 10 rounds from
the pastry using a 9cm cutter
and press into muffin holes.

2 eggs
100ml single cream
100g feta cheese

Using a hand whisk, whisk eggs
and cream together. Divide the
pumpkin between muffin holes
and top with equally divided egg
mixture then sprinkle with feta.

Bake for 15-20 minutes until
golden.

ROASTED PEPPER RISOTTO

Roasted Pepper Risotto

Serves 6

1 onion, finely chopped
3 red peppers, deseeded and diced
75g butter
400g risotto rice

1.5 litre hot vegetable or chicken stock
75g Parmesan cheese, grated

Preheat grill to medium.

Fry the onion and peppers gently in the butter in a large pan until they are soft. Add the rice and stir together until the rice grains are coated all over.

Add the first ladleful of hot stock and stir it in. When it is absorbed add a further ladleful. Continue in this way for 25-30 minutes until the risotto is creamy and rice is tender, add the Parmesan and stir through.

Note: If you wish use a jar of red peppers instead of the fresh. Just make sure you drain them well.

SPEEDY
NACHOS

Simply 3 - 5

Speedy Nachos v

Serves 2-3

200g bag plain tortilla chips
2-3 spring onions, sliced
75g Cheddar cheese,
jalapenos, as many as you like

300g jar salsa

Preheat grill to medium.

Put tortilla chips on baking sheet
and sprinkle with onions, cheese,
and jalapenos.
Grill until cheese is melted.

Top with salsa and put back
under grill until just warm.

TOMATO, CAULIFLOWER AND SPINACH CURRY

Tomato, Cauliflower and Spinach Curry v

Serves 4

1 onion, sliced
2 tbsp oil
2 tbsp curry paste

Fry the onion in the oil for about 7 minutes until soft and golden. Add the curry paste and cook for a couple of minutes until fragrant.

1 small cauliflower, cut into bite sized florets
400g can chopped tomatoes
300ml water

Add the cauliflower, tomato and the water and bring to a gentle simmer for 15-20 minutes until the tomato has broken down and the cauliflower is tender.

100g spinach, roughly chopped

Stir in the spinach until wilted.

TOMATO AND RICOTTA TARTS

Tomato and Ricotta Tarts

Serves 8

150g prosciutto

500g ricotta cheese
1 egg
8 cherry tomatoes
4 tsp basil pesto

Preheat oven to 180°C.

Lightly grease 8 holes in a muffin pan and line with slices of prosciutto ensuring base and sides are lined.

Mash the ricotta with the egg. Divide the ricotta mixture evenly into muffin holes. Cut tomatoes in half and push into top of tart. Top with ½ teaspoon of pesto.

Bake for about 25 minutes until firm.

VEGETABLE PESTO PASTRIES

Vegetable Pesto Pastries v

Serves 4

2 sheets frozen ready rolled puff pastry, thawed

5 tbsp sundried tomato pesto

280g jar antipasto chargrilled vegetables

4 plum tomatoes, sliced lengthways
150g feta cheese, crumbled

Preheat oven to 200°C.

Cut the pastry in half. Place the four pastry pieces onto two baking sheets. Fold the pastry edges in to make a 1cm border.

Spread the pesto over the centre of the pastry within the border.

Drain the vegetables and pat dry with kitchen paper. Cut the vegetables into strips.

Arrange the tomato slices on the pastry pieces and place vegetables on top of the tomatoes. Sprinkle with the cheese. Bake for 10 minutes or until the pastry is puffed and golden.

Note: Use sliced ordinary tomatoes if you don't have plum tomatoes.

Simply 3 - 5

Beef

BEEF CASSEROLE WITH MOROCCAN SPICE

Beef Casserole with Moroccan Spice

Serves 6

1kg casserole steak
2 tbsp Ras El Hanout

1-2 tbsp vegetable oil

750ml beef stock
400g can chopped tomatoes
400g can chickpeas, drained
and rinsed

Preheat oven to 180°C.

Cut beef into 3cm cubes and place in a large bowl. Add the Ras El Hanout and mix well.

Heat the oil in a frying pan and fry the beef in 2 or 3 batches to brown. Remove each batch and place in a casserole dish.

Pour the stock into the frying pan and bring to the boil, stirring. Add to the casserole with the tomatoes and chickpeas and stir to combine.

Cover the casserole dish and cook for about 2 hours or until beef is very tender. Stir every 40 minutes or so and if it is drying out add a little water.

Note: The secret to making any casserole is to brown the meat well first. Ras El Hanout is a Moroccan spice mix which you can buy at supermarkets.

Serve this with rice or noodles.

BEEF
GOULASH

Beef Goulash

Serves 4-6

1 tbsp vegetable oil
2 small onions,
chopped into large pieces
1 kg casserole steak, cubed

Heat the oil in a saucepan and fry the onions and beef browning the beef on all sides.

1 clove garlic, finely chopped
4 tsp mild or hot paprika
1 x 400g can chopped tomatoes

Add the garlic, paprika and tomatoes. Cook, covered with a lid, over a low heat for about an hour or until the beef is tender.

Note: Use mild or hot paprika depending on how hot you like your food.

BEEF
MADRAS

Beef Madras

Serves 4

2 tbsp vegetable oil
2 medium onions, diced

140g Madras curry paste
500g topside or rump
400g tomatoes, chopped
200ml water

Heat the oil in a saucepan and fry onions until they are golden.

Stir in curry paste and beef then add in tomatoes and water.

Simmer over a low heat for about 40 minutes or until the beef is cooked.

Note: We use Patak's curry paste and it is about ½ the jar. This also works well with chicken or lamb. If you wish use canned tomatoes but we prefer fresh tomatoes.

BEEF WITH PEAS AND BLACK BEAN SAUCE

Simply 3 - 5

Beef with Peas and Black Bean Sauce

Serves 4

2 tbsp vegetable oil 350g rump steak, cut into thin slices	Heat the oil in a wok or large frying pan. Add the steak and stir fry for 2 minutes.
1 onion, sliced 2 cloves garlic, crushed 150g frozen peas	Add the onion, garlic and peas to the wok and stir fry for a further 5 minutes.
195g jar black bean sauce	Add the black bean sauce and heat through for a further 2 minutes. Note: Serve with rice or noodles.

HONEY MUSTARD BEEF STIR FRY

Honey Mustard Beef Stir Fry

Serves 4

1 tbsp vegetable oil
2 onions, cut into wedges
650g rump or topside,
cut into fine slices

5 tbsp Dijon mustard
4 tbsp honey
250g mangetout

Heat a deep frying pan or wok over a high heat. Add the oil and onions and cook for 2 minutes. Add the beef slices and cook for 4 minutes or until well browned.

Add the mustard, honey and mangetout and toss to coat. Cook for a further 2-3 minutes or until the mangetout are just tender. Add a little water if required.

Note: Serve with rice or noodles.

MINI BEEF WELLINGTONS

Simply 3 - 5

Mini Beef Wellingtons

Serves 4

4 fillet steaks, brushed with
a little oil
4 tbsp mushroom pate

2 x 375g ready rolled puff pastry,
each cut into 4 (you will have 8
pieces of pastry)
1 egg, beaten

Preheat the oven to 200°C.

Fry the steaks for about 30
seconds each side just to sear.
Cool slightly then top each
steak with pate.

Place each steak on a piece of
pastry and brush around the
edge with a little of the beaten
egg. Lay another piece of
pastry on top and press the
edges together firmly. Trim
leaving a border and press
again to make sure the edges
are sealed.

Brush with the egg and bake for
about 10 minutes for medium
rare.

Note: You can buy mushroom
pate ready made.

PEPPERED STEAK

Peppered Steak

Serves 4

pepper
4 rump steaks
olive oil, for rubbing steak

Using a pepper grinder, grind enough pepper to coat a plate. Rub the steak with olive oil and coat in the pepper.

Heat 1 tablespoon of olive oil in a frying pan over a medium heat, cook the steak for about 3 minutes on each side or until cooked to your liking. Transfer to a plate and rest for 5 minutes.

80ml brandy
240ml double cream
150ml vegetable stock or water
5 tbsp finely chopped
flat leaf parsley

Heat the same frying pan, add the brandy and stir for 30 seconds. Pour in the cream and stock and bring to the boil. Reduce heat and simmer for 1 minute or until sauce has thickened then stir in the parsley and serve over steak.

PESTO BURGERS

Simply 3 - 5

Pesto Burgers

Serves 4

500g lean minced beef
2 tbsp water
80ml basil pesto
½ onion, finely diced

Combine the mince, water,
pesto and onion. Mix until
well combined and shape into
4 burgers.

Heat a frying pan on a medium
heat. Lightly brush the burgers
with oil and cook burgers on
each side for 6-7 minutes or until
cooked through.

Pasta Burgers

ROAST RIB OF BEEF WITH GRAVY

Roast Rib of Beef with Gravy

Serves 6

rib of beef or sirloin of beef
approx 1.5kg
1 tbsp plain flour
1 tbsp mustard powder
2 small onions

Gravy
25g plain flour
1 litre vegetable stock
or potato water

Preheat oven to 220°C.

Rub surface of meat with combined flour and mustard powder. Cut onions in half and place in roasting tin, pop meat on top. The onions will caramelise and add flavour and colour to the gravy.

Cook for 20 minutes at this temperature and then lower temperature to 180°C. See note for cooking time.

Remove meat from tin (discard onions) and allow meat to stand for at least 30 minutes, covered in foil, before carving. This makes for easier carving.

Pour out all but 2 tablespoons of the fat from the roasting tin. Place the tin on the heat and using a hand whisk, stir in the flour. When you have a smooth paste start to add the liquid slowly and continue to whisk until it comes to the boil. Allow to reduce a little.

Note: Cook for 15 minutes to each 500g for rare meat. Add about 15 minutes to the total cooking time for medium rare and 30 minutes for well done.

SIRLOIN STEAK WITH CHUNKY CHIPS

Sirloin Steak with Chunky Chips

Serves 2

Preheat oven to 180°C.

500g potatoes
2 tbsp olive oil

Scrub the potatoes but you don't need to peel them. Cut into thick chips then dry the chips with kitchen paper and place into a roasting tin. Drizzle over the olive oil and shake the tin to coat the potatoes. Roast for about 40 minutes, shaking the tin halfway through the cooking time.

2 sirloin steaks
olive oil, for rubbing steaks

Rub the steaks with a little olive oil.

100g crème fraiche
2 tbsp horseradish sauce
2 tbsp snipped fresh chives

Mix the crème fraiche, horseradish and half the chives.

When the chips are almost done, heat the grill to high and grill the steaks for 2-3 minutes on each side depending on how you like them and how thick they are. If you prefer you can fry the steaks.

Serve with a pile of chips, a dollop of horseradish cream and sprinkle over remaining chives.

POULTRY

Simply 3 - 5

Poultry

CHICKEN BREASTS WITH CITRUS GLAZE

Chicken Breasts with Citrus Glaze

Serves 4

3 oranges

Using a potato peeler cut thin strips of rind from 1 orange avoiding the white pith. Cut strips into matchstick size pieces. Squeeze the juice from the oranges, you will need 250ml, and set aside.

1 tbsp olive oil
4 chicken breasts, skinless

Heat the oil in a large frying pan and cook chicken until browned on both sides. Reduce heat and cook, covered, until chicken is cooked through. Remove from pan and keep warm.

125ml chicken stock
125ml sweet orange marmalade

Add the orange juice, stock and marmalade to the same pan and stir until marmalade melts. Add rind, bring to the boil then simmer for approximately 10 minutes, uncovered, or until sauce has thickened slightly.

Return chicken to the pan, coat with glaze then serve.

Note: You can use skinless thigh fillets if you prefer.

CHICKEN WITH WILD MUSHROOM AND CREAM SAUCE

Simply 3 - 5

Chicken with Wild Mushroom and Cream Sauce

Serves 6

1 large chicken

Mushroom Sauce

300g mixed wild mushrooms, sliced or quartered
450ml fresh chicken stock
150ml double cream
3 tbsp roughly chopped tarragon

Preheat oven to 190°C.

Put the chicken in a roasting tin and roast for 1½-2 hours depending on size of chicken. Transfer the roast chicken to a warm plate and cover loosely with foil.

Pour off all but 1 tablespoon of fat from the roasting tin and put tin on the stovetop. Fry the mushrooms in this for 2 minutes until lightly browned. Add the stock and simmer, scraping bottom of pan, until reduced by half. Stir in the cream and bring just to the boil, then stir in the tarragon.

GREEN CHICKEN CURRY

Green Chicken Curry

Serves 4

200g green beans, cut into bite size pieces	Add the green beans to boiling water and simmer for a couple of minutes until just tender.
1 tbsp olive oil 3 tbsp green curry paste 600g chicken thighs, skinless and thinly sliced	Heat the oil in a saucepan or wok. Add the curry paste and chicken and stir fry for about 5 minutes or until the chicken is just cooked.
250ml coconut milk 1 tsp brown sugar	Add the coconut milk, green beans and sugar and stir fry for about 5 minutes.

HONEYED DUCK

Honeyed Duck

Serves 4

Preheat oven to 200°C.

4 medium duck breasts, skin on

Prick duck skin all over with a fork and transfer to a wire rack set over a roasting tin (allows fat to drip away).

1 tbsp soy sauce
1 tbsp honey

Put soy sauce and honey in a small bowl and mix well. Spread mixture over duck skin.

Transfer to the oven and cook for 15-20 minutes until duck skin is crispy and meat is still pink in the middle. Let rest for 5 minutes before carving and serving.

MEDITERRANEAN
CHICKEN

Simply 3 - 5

Mediterranean Chicken

Serves 4

2 tbsp olive oil
8 chicken thigh fillets

Heat half the oil in a flameproof casserole pan and add chicken. Cook until chicken is golden on both sides. Remove from the pan and place on a plate.

1 medium onion, cut into wedges
1 red pepper, sliced
400g jar arrabbiata pasta sauce
about 30 pitted kalamata olives

Add the remaining oil to the pan and cook the onion and pepper, stirring, for 4-5 minutes until onion has softened. Return the chicken to the pan then add pasta sauce and olives. Cover and bring gently to the boil. Reduce heat and simmer, turning chicken occasionally, for about 30 minutes or until chicken is cooked through.

PANCETTA CHICKEN

Pancetta Chicken

Serves 4

1 tbsp grated lemon rind
2 cloves garlic, crushed
2 tbsp chopped flat leaf parsley
8 large chicken thighs, boned
8 slices pancetta or bacon

Preheat oven to 190°C.

Mix rind, garlic and parsley together and rub into the inside of each thigh. Roll up and wrap in slices of pancetta or bacon. Cook in oven for about 30 minutes or until cooked through.

Note: This is good to serve as part of a roast dinner as no carving is involved.

ROAST DUCK WITH RED WINE SAUCE

Roast Duck
with Red Wine Sauce

Serves 4

2 cloves garlic
4 duck legs
¼ tsp five spice powder

300ml red wine
2 tbsp redcurrant jelly

Preheat oven to 170°C.

Put the garlic cloves on the bottom of a roasting tin and place the duck legs on top. Sprinkle with the five spice powder and roast for 1 hour.

Bring the wine and redcurrant jelly to the boil and then simmer gently for about 4 minutes.

When the duck has cooked for the 1 hour remove it from the oven and spoon off all the fat. Pour the wine mixture around the duck and return to the oven and cook for a further 15-20 minutes to finish cooking the duck and reduce the sauce.

ROSEMARY, BRIE AND SUNDRIED TOMATO CHICKEN

Rosemary, Brie and Sundried Tomato Chicken

Serves 2

30g sundried tomatoes, finely chopped
1 tbsp finely chopped rosemary leaves
60g firm Brie, finely chopped

2 chicken breasts

Preheat oven to 180°C.

Combine tomato, rosemary and Brie in a small bowl.

Slit a pocket in 1 side of each chicken breast (don't cut all the way through). Divide the tomato mixture between the pockets and secure with a toothpick.

Put in a small roasting tin and roast for 25-30 minutes or until cooked through.

TURKEY BURGER

Turkey Burger

Serves 4

450g minced turkey
1 tbsp chopped thyme leaves
3 tbsp breadcrumbs
1 egg, lightly beaten

1 tbsp olive oil

In a bowl combine turkey, thyme, breadcrumbs and egg. Mix well with your hands and form the mixture into four balls then flatten into patties.

Heat the oil in a frying pan and fry the burgers for about 4-5 minutes on both sides until brown and cooked through.

FISH

Simply 3 - 5

Fish

Calamari 165
Serves 2 for lunch or 4 as a starter

Chilli and Lime Tuna Steaks 167
Serves 4

Herb Crusted Baked Haddock 169
Serves 2

Mussels with Garlic, Vermouth and Parsley 171
Serves 4

Pan Fried Salmon with Hollandaise 173
Serves 2

Salmon and Pea Fish Cakes 175
Serves 4

Seared Scallops with Crushed Potatoes 177
Serves 2 for lunch or 4 as a starter

Trout with Watercress Sauce 179
Serves 2

CALAMARI

Calamari

Serves 2 for lunch or 4 as a starter

250g squid

Tempura Batter
1 egg
125ml iced water
75g plain flour, sifted
½ tsp bicarbonate of soda

Slice the body of the squid into rings and the tentacles into small pieces.

Using a whisk, lightly mix together egg, water, flour and bicarbonate of soda until smooth. Do not over mix.

Heat oil to 190°C, dip squid in batter and fry in batches for about 1 minute.

Note: Can be served with the Tartare Sauce in Sauce Section.

CHILLI AND LIME TUNA STEAKS

Chilli and Lime Tuna Steaks

Serves 4

20g fresh coriander
1 large red chilli, deseeded and
finely sliced
2 shallots, finely sliced
1 lime, grated zest and juice

4 tuna steaks

Reserve a little of the coriander for the garnish and roughly chop the rest. Put in a small bowl along with the chilli, shallots, lime zest and juice.

Using your fingers rub this mixture over the tuna steaks. Leave to marinate for 20 minutes.

Cook the tuna steaks for 2-3 minutes on each side. Garnish with coriander leaves.

Note: These can be cooked on the barbecue or in an oiled frying pan.

HERB CRUSTED BAKED HADDOCK

Herb Crusted Baked Haddock

Serves 2

2 x 200g haddock fillets

100g fresh breadcrumbs
1 tbsp chopped parsley
1 tbsp chopped coriander
1 tbsp finely chopped chives

50g butter, melted

Preheat oven to 180°C.

Place haddock fillets on a lightly greased baking sheet.

Mix breadcrumbs, parsley, coriander and chives.
Place onto haddock covering each fillet completely.

Drizzle the butter over the breadcrumbs and bake fish in the oven for 15-18 minutes or until the haddock is cooked.

MUSSELS WITH GARLIC, VERMOUTH AND PARSLEY

Simply 3 - 5

Mussels with Garlic, Vermouth and Parsley

Serves 4

1kg mussels in shell

50g butter
150ml dry vermouth
2 cloves garlic, crushed
handful of chopped flat leaf parsley

Preheat oven to 200°C.

Scrub mussels clean, pull off beards and discard any mussels that are cracked or don't close when tapped. (These are dead and therefore should not be eaten).

Fold 4 60x30cm pieces of foil in half lengthways and divide butter, vermouth, garlic, parsley and mussels between them. Bring corners of each piece of foil together to close the parcel leaving a space in each one so mussels can open. Pinch edges to seal.

Put parcels on baking sheet and cook in oven for 10-12 minutes or until mussels have opened (check 1 of the parcels). Any mussels that don't open should be discarded.

Put parcels in warmed bowls and serve with crusty bread.

PAN FRIED SALMON WITH HOLLANDAISE

Simply 3 - 5

Pan Fried Salmon with Hollandaise

Serves 2

8 asparagus spears, ends trimmed
2 handfuls of broad beans, popped out of their pods

Cook asparagus and broad beans separately in boiling water for 2-3 minutes until just cooked through.

1 tbsp olive oil
2 salmon fillets

Heat oil in a frying pan and cook salmon skin side down for 4 minutes and then turn and cook for a further 1-2 minutes until cooked through.

jar of hollandaise sauce

Serve salmon on top of vegetables and then spoon sauce over.

Note: Broad beans come in an outer pod and then each bean has an outer shell. If you pop them out of the outer shell they will be much tastier. If you can't get broad beans just use extra asparagus.

SALMON AND PEA FISH CAKES

Salmon and Pea Fish Cakes

Serves 4

418g can red or pink salmon, drained
140g frozen peas, defrosted
1 tbsp tartare sauce
500g mashed potatoes
3 tbsp plain flour, approx

Flake the salmon into a bowl, removing any skin and large bones. Add the peas, tartare and potato and mix well. Using floured hands shape into 8 flat fish cakes and dust each with a little flour.

3 tbsp vegetable oil

Heat oil in a large frying pan over a medium heat. Fry the fish cakes in 2 batches for about 4 minutes each side, turning carefully with a fish slice until golden and crisp.

SEARED SCALLOPS WITH CRUSHED POTATOES

Seared Scallops with Crushed Potatoes

Serves 2 for lunch or 4 as a starter

500g new potatoes, peeled
1 tbsp extra virgin olive oil
25g pitted black olives, chopped
1 tbsp chopped flat leaf parsley

12 large scallops
2 tbsp extra virgin olive oil

Cook potatoes in boiling water until just tender. Drain well and return to pan. Lightly crush with a fork, add olive oil, olives and parsley.

Put scallops in bowl, add olive oil and toss to coat. Sear scallops in a hot pan for about 1 minute each side. Remove from pan and rest for 30 seconds.

Pile potatoes on plate and top with scallops.

TROUT WITH WATERCRESS SAUCE

Trout with Watercress Sauce

Serves 2

2 trout fillets

100g watercress, roughly chopped
200g low fat fromage frais
2 tbsp capers, rinsed and chopped
juice of ½ lemon

Heat the oven to 180°C.

Put the trout on a piece of oiled foil, and fold up to make a parcel. Cook in the oven for 10-15 minutes or until cooked through.

Meanwhile, process the watercress with the fromage frais in a food processor. Stir in the capers and lemon juice.

Serve the trout with the sauce.

LAMB

Simply 3 - 5

Lamb

FRENCH LAMB CHOP CASSEROLE

French Lamb Chop Casserole

Serves 4

1 tbsp vegetable oil
8 lean lamb chump chops

6 baby onions, halved
2 cloves garlic, crushed
2 small leeks, chopped
40g French onion soup mix
375ml boiling water

Preheat oven to 180°C.

Heat the oil in a flameproof casserole dish. Fry the lamb in batches until browned on each side. Remove from dish.

Cook onions, garlic and leeks in same dish, stirring, until the onions are browned slightly. Return the lamb to the dish, sprinkle with the soup mix and pour the water over the top.

Bake in the oven, covered, for about 40 minutes. Uncover for the last 10 minutes if sauce needs to thicken.

GREEK STYLE ROAST LAMB

Greek Style Roast Lamb

erves 6-8

Preheat the oven to 200°C.

x 2kg leg of lamb
large cloves garlic,
ut into thin slices

Cut small slits all over the lamb
and insert slices of garlic.

tbsp olive oil
tbsp dried oregano

Mix the olive oil and oregano.
Using your hand, rub the
mixture all over the lamb.

00ml dry white wine, approx

Place the lamb in a large
roasting tin and pour in enough
wine to cover the base. Roast
in the oven for 20 minutes then
reduce the oven temperature to
180°C and cook for a further 1½
hours. Allow the lamb to rest
for 15 minutes before carving.

squeeze of lemon juice

Skim most of the fat from the
juices left in the tin and whisk
in a squeeze of lemon juice.
Reheat the sauce and serve over
the sliced lamb.

LAMB
KORMA

Lamb Korma

Serves 4-6

tbsp vegetable oil
800g diced lamb

clove garlic, finely chopped
tbsp garam masala

2 x 400g cans chopped tomatoes
200ml natural yoghurt

Heat the oil in a saucepan and fry the lamb browning on all sides.

Add the garlic and garam masala and stir for two minutes.

Add the tomatoes and yoghurt and cook, covered, over a low heat for an hour.

Note: If you prefer transfer to a casserole dish and cook in the oven at 170°C for about an hour.

LAMB MEATBALLS

Lamb Meatballs

Serves 4

500g minced lamb
2 tbsp chopped fresh mint
35g stale breadcrumbs
1 egg, lightly beaten
2 tbsp sesame seeds, toasted

vegetable oil, for shallow frying

Combine all the ingredients
in a bowl.

Roll 2 level teaspoons of
mixture into balls.

Shallow fry in hot oil
until brown and cooked through.
Drain on kitchen paper.

LAMB TIKKA CUTLETS

Lamb Tikka Cutlets

Serves 4-6

12 lamb cutlets
125ml tikka paste
2 tbsp natural yoghurt

1 tbsp vegetable oil

Combine the lamb cutlets, paste and yoghurt in a large bowl. Cover and refrigerate for at least 15 minutes.

Heat the oil in a large non stick frying pan. Fry the cutlets until browned on both sides and cooked to your liking.

LAMB WITH CHILLI TOMATOES

Simply 3 - 5

Lamb with Chilli Tomatoes

Serves 2

140g ripe vine tomatoes, halved, seeds removed and flesh finely chopped
½ small red onion, finely chopped
½ fresh red chilli, deseeded and finely chopped
1 tbsp chopped coriander

Mix the tomatoes, onion, chilli and coriander in a bowl. This can now be left in the fridge for several hours, but make sure it is at room temperature when you serve it.

2 lamb leg steaks
olive oil, for brushing

Brush the lamb with some olive oil. Barbecue or grill for 3-4 minutes each side or until cooked to your liking. Serve with the chilli tomatoes.

MUSTARD GLAZED RACK OF LAMB

Mustard Glazed Rack of Lamb

Serves 6

3 racks of lamb, trimmed of most
of the fat

3 tbsp cider or dry white wine
3 tbsp honey flavoured mustard
rosemary sprigs

Preheat the oven to 180°C.

Score the fat on the lamb in a
criss cross pattern and place in
a small roasting tin.

Mix the cider or wine with the
mustard and spread some of
the glaze over the lamb. Place a
couple of sprigs of rosemary on
each rack of lamb and roast in
the oven, brushing occasionally
with the rest of the glaze, for
about 30 minutes or until cooked
to your liking.

Note: If you have any difficulty
getting honey flavoured
mustard use 1 tbsp honey and 2
tbsp mustard.

RED LAMB CURRY

Red Lamb Curry

Serves 4

1 tbsp vegetable oil 700g lamb fillet, cut into strips	Heat the oil in a large frying pan. Cook the lamb in batches until browned. Remove from the pan and set aside.
2 medium onions, sliced	Add the onion to the same pan and cook for 3-4 minutes.
1 large red pepper, sliced 4 tbsp red curry paste 400ml coconut milk	Add the pepper and curry paste and cook, stirring, until onion is soft. Return the lamb to the pan with the coconut milk. Stir until heated through.

PASTA SAUCES

Simply 3 - 5

Pasta Sauces

BOLOGNESE PASTA SAUCE

Bolognese Pasta Sauce

Serves 4

1 tbsp olive oil
2 onions, finely chopped
2 cloves garlic, crushed
500g lean minced beef

Heat the oil in a large frying pan. Cook the onions, and garlic for 5-8 minutes until soft. Add the minced beef and cook for 5 minutes until brown and cooked through.

500g jar pasta sauce
1 tbsp Worcestershire sauce

Add the pasta sauce and Worcestershire sauce. Cover and simmer for about 35 minutes, stirring from time to time.

Note: We use different pasta sauces such as mushroom pasta sauce. Use whichever one you like.

CARBONARA PASTA SAUCE

Simply 3 - 5

Carbonara Pasta Sauce

Serves 4

125ml olive oil
150g pancetta, cubed

Heat the oil in a large frying pan over a medium to high heat. Add the pancetta and cook, stirring often, until golden. Add the pancetta and oil to cooked, drained spaghetti.

2 egg yolks
1 whole egg
50ml milk

Whisk the eggs with the milk and stir into the spaghetti.

100g Parmesan cheese

Add the Parmesan cheese and serve.

Note: Use bacon instead of the pancetta if you prefer.

CORIANDER CHILLI AND LIME PASTA SAUCE

CREAMY ROASTED PEPPER PASTA SAUCE

Simply 3 - 5

Coriander, Chilli and Lime Pasta Sauce v

Serves 2-3

30g fresh coriander leaves
2 tbsp olive oil
1 tbsp salted roasted peanuts
1 red chilli, seeded and diced
2 tbsp lime juice

Process ingredients until well combined. Stir through cooked pasta.

Note: As well as serving this as a pasta sauce it is also lovely if you brush it onto fish or chicken and then grill the fish or chicken.

Creamy Roasted Pepper Pasta Sauce v

Serves 4

2 tbsp oil
2 cloves garlic, sliced
1 x 280g jar red peppers, drained and diced

200ml carton half fat crème fraiche
2 tsp wholegrain mustard
85g Cheddar cheese, grated

Heat the oil and gently fry the garlic for 1 minute. Add the drained peppers and heat through.

Stir in crème fraiche, mustard and cheese and heat gently until cheese has melted. Stir through cooked pasta.

NAPOLETANA PASTA SAUCE

Napoletana Pasta Sauce v

Serves 4

1kg plum tomatoes

Plunge the tomatoes in boiling water for about 30 seconds then cool in cold water. Peel and cut into small pieces.

4 tbsp olive oil
2 cloves garlic, crushed
15 basil leaves, chopped
½ tsp sugar

Combine the oil and garlic in a large saucepan and fry over a high heat until the garlic is just golden. Add the tomatoes, basil and sugar and cook for 10 minutes.

1 tbsp tomato paste

Add the tomato paste and cook for a further 2 minutes.

Note: This sauce is very light and fresh. If you prefer a more robust sauce just add tomato paste to taste. You can use ordinary tomatoes if you can't get plum tomatoes.

SMOKED SALMON AND HORSERADISH PASTA SAUCE

SUNDRIED TOMATO PESTO PASTA SAUCE

Simply 3 - 5

Smoked Salmon and Horseradish Pasta Sauce

Serves 2

150g smoked salmon, cut into strips
1 lemon, zested and juiced
75g of watercress
2 tbsp horseradish sauce
2 tbsp crème fraiche

Mix all the ingredients together and stir through cooked pasta.

Sundried Tomato Pesto Pasta Sauce v

Serves 4

40g pine nuts

Toast the pine nuts carefully in a dry frying pan. Remove from the pan and let them cool.

1 x 280g jar sundried tomatoes
25g Parmesan cheese, grated

Drain the tomatoes (reserving the oil) and place tomatoes, pine nuts and Parmesan in a food processor. Process until fairly fine and then slowly drizzle in the reserved oil to form a thick paste.

Note: This is lovely used as a pasta sauce or just served with crusty bread.

TOMATO, BACON AND GOAT'S CHEESE PASTA SAUCE

TOMATO, LEMON AND FETA PASTA SAUCE

Simply 3 - 5

Tomato, Bacon and Goat's Cheese Pasta Sauce

Serves 2

2 tbsp olive oil
100g diced bacon or pancetta
2 cloves garlic, chopped
4 large ripe tomatoes, skinned and each cut into 8

Heat 1 tablespoon of the oil and add bacon or pancetta. Fry until crisp then add garlic, tomatoes and the rest of the oil. Heat for about 3 minutes until just simmering. Add this to cooked pasta.

50g soft goat's cheese
handful of fresh basil leaves, torn

Serve with cheese and basil leaves scattered over.

Tomato, Lemon and Feta Pasta Sauce v

Serves 4

2 tbsp olive oil
500g courgettes,
halved lengthways and sliced
2 cloves garlic, thinly sliced

Heat the oil a large saucepan and fry the courgettes and garlic for 3-4 minutes until softened.

finely grated zest of 1 lemon
6 ripe tomatoes, roughly chopped

Add the lemon zest, tomatoes and about 3 tablespoons of water. Cook for a further 3 minutes until the tomatoes begin to soften.

140g feta cheese, crumbled
juice of 1 lemon

Remove from the heat stir in the cheese, stir through cooked pasta, and add lemon juice to taste.

PORK

Simply 3 - 5

Pork

CHINESE ROAST PORK

Chinese Roast Pork

Serves 4

1kg belly pork slices
1 tbsp salt
3 tsp Chinese five spice powder

Wash and dry the belly pork. Combine the salt and five spice powder and rub it all over the skin and meat. Leave in fridge for at least 2 hours.

Heat the oven to 210°C. Bake for 20 minutes.

Lower the oven setting to 180°C and bake for a further 20 minutes or until the skin crackles and crisps.

4 tbsp hoisin sauce

Serve warm with hoisin sauce for dipping.

Note: The salt is essential in this recipe to help the pork crisp.

HAWAIIAN PORK CHOPS

Simply 3 - 5

Hawaiian Pork Chops

Serves 4

Preheat oven to 180°C.

4 large pork chops

Place chops in large ovenproof baking dish.

225g pineapple pieces in natural juices, drained
2 tsp dried oregano
2 tomatoes, finely chopped
120g grated Cheddar cheese

Mix together pineapple, oregano and tomatoes. Spoon mixture onto chops. Sprinkle with cheese. Bake chops for 25-30 minutes or until cooked through.

LEG OF PORK WITH PORK WITH PROSCIUTTO AND APPLES

Leg of Pork with Prosciutto and Apples

Serves 8

3 apples, cored and cut
into quarters
6 slices prosciutto
2kg leg of pork

Preheat oven to 180°C.

Arrange the apples in an oven dish. Wrap the prosciutto slices over the underside of the leg of pork and place on top of the apples. Cover with foil and roast for 1 hour.

Remove the foil and cook for a further 1 hour.

Turn the oven temperature up to 220°C and cook for about 20-25 minutes or until pork is cooked through and crackling is crispy.

Allow to rest 15 minutes before slicing and serving with the prosciutto and apple on the side.

PARMA WRAPPED PORK TENDERLOIN

Simply 3 - 5

Parma Wrapped Pork Tenderloin

Serves 6

200g Parma ham
100g sage leaves

2 pork tenderloins

Preheat oven to 180°C.

Lay half the Parma ham on a sheet of clingfilm. Lay half the sage leaves on top of the ham.

Lay one tenderloin on top of the sage and wrap the ham around the pork. Form into a sausage shape using the clingfilm. Repeat with the other tenderloin.

Just prior to cooking unwrap the clingfilm and place the pork in a roasting tin. Cook in the oven for 15-20 minutes or until pork is cooked through.

Allow to stand for 3-4 minutes before carving.

Note: This looks good if you cut on the diagonal to serve.

PORK AND APRICOT BURGERS

Pork and Apricot Burgers

Serves 4

500g minced pork
4 spring onions, finely chopped
2 tbsp chopped fresh mint
2 fresh apricots, roughly chopped
1 egg beaten

Mix together the pork, spring onions, mint and apricots. Season well and bind together with the beaten egg.

Divide the mixture into four then shape into burgers.

Grill the burgers under a medium heat or fry in 1 tablespoon of oil 8-10 minutes each side.

PORK AND MUSHROOM STROGANOFF

Pork and Mushroom Stroganoff

Serves 4

450g pork fillet
2 tbsp plain flour

Cut the pork into strips. Coat in the flour and shake off any excess.

15g butter
1 tbsp oil
6 shallots, quartered

Heat the butter and oil in a large frying pan, add the shallots and cook for about 5 minutes until golden. Remove from the pan.

225g button mushrooms, sliced thickly

Add the pork to the frying pan and cook, stirring, for about 5 minutes. Return the shallots to the frying pan along with the mushrooms. Cook for a few more minutes until the pork is cooked through.

250ml crème fraiche

Reduce the heat and stir in the crème fraiche. Heat gently for a few minutes, but don't allow to boil.

PORK CHOPS WITH CIDER AND CREAM

Pork Chops with Cider and Cream

Serves 4

1 tbsp olive oil
4 pork chops, rind snipped off
1 onion, sliced

Heat the oil in a frying pan then fry the chops until browned. Remove, add the onion and cook for about 10 minutes until soft and caramelised.

200ml cider
150ml double cream
1 tbsp wholegrain mustard

Add the cider, bring to a simmer and reduce a little. Add the cream and mustard, stir, bring to a simmer then put the chops back in and cook for 8-10 minutes or until cooked through.

PORK RIBS WITH BBQ SAUCE

Pork Ribs with BBQ Sauce

Serves 4

450g pork spare ribs

BBQ Sauce

4 tbsp tomato ketchup
1 tbsp black treacle
3-4 tbsp lemon juice
2 tsp hoisin sauce

Preheat the oven to 190°C.

Place spare ribs in a casserole dish with a lid. Put in the oven for 45-50 minutes.

Towards the end of the cooking time put the ketchup, treacle, juice and hoisin sauce in a saucepan. Whisk together and heat through (you can do this in a microwave if you prefer).

Remove the ribs from the oven and drain off the juices. Pour the BBQ sauce over the ribs and return the dish to the oven for a further 30 minutes, uncovered.

Baste the ribs once during this time.

PORK STEAKS WITH MUSTARD SAUCE

Pork Steaks with Mustard Sauce

Serves 2

25g butter
1 tbsp olive oil
1 large clove garlic, halved
2 pork steaks

Heat the butter and oil in a frying pan. Cook the garlic for 1-2 minutes until soft then add in the pork steaks. Cook over a medium heat on both sides until brown and cooked through. Discard the garlic and put the pork on a plate, cover with foil, and allow to rest.

2 tbsp chopped flat leaf parsley
225ml double cream
3 tbsp Dijon mustard

Pour away all but 1 tablespoon of the oil in the pan and add the parsley and cream. Stir in the mustard and gently bring to the boil, stirring. Simmer for about 4 minutes, then serve over steaks.

SAUSAGES WITH MUSTARD AND APPLE SAUCE

Sausages with Mustard and Apple Sauce

Serves 4

1 tbsp vegetable oil
8 herb flavoured pork sausages
2 eating apples, cored and each cut into 8 wedges

Heat the oil in a large frying pan, add the sausages and fry for about 8 minutes turning often to brown. Add in the apples and continue to fry until apples are golden, stirring carefully so that the apples don't break up.

1 tbsp redcurrant jelly
300ml chicken stock
2 tbsp wholegrain mustard

Stir the redcurrant jelly into the stock and mix well then stir in the mustard. Pour this into the frying pan and allow to boil for a few minutes to make a syrupy sauce.

Lower the heat and gently simmer, uncovered, for 10 minutes or until the sausages are cooked through.

SIDE DISHES

Simply 3 - 5

Side Dishes

SIDE DISHES

Simply 3 - 5
Side Dishes

ALMOND CORIANDER COUSCOUS

Almond Coriander Couscous

Serves 4

70g flaked almonds	Toast the almonds gently in a frying pan.
500ml chicken stock 400g couscous 20g butter	Bring the stock to the boil in a saucepan and stir in the couscous and butter. Remove the pan from the heat, stand, covered, for about 5 minutes.
4 tbsp coarsely chopped fresh coriander	Fluff up with a fork and gently toss the almonds and coriander through the couscous.

ASPARAGUS WITH BUTTER AND LEMON SAUCE

Asparagus with Butter and Lemon Sauce v

Serves 2

300g asparagus, stalks trimmed

Place the asparagus in a microwave safe container with a teaspoon of water. Microwave on High, 3 minutes for crisp asparagus, 5 minutes for soft asparagus.

40g butter
1 tbsp lemon juice

Meanwhile in a small saucepan heat the butter and lemon juice together until simmering. Pour sauce over the asparagus and serve.

BALSAMIC GLAZED CARROTS

Balsamic Glazed Carrots v

Serves 4-6

2 bunches baby carrots,
trimmed and scrubbed

45g brown sugar
15g melted butter
1 tbsp balsamic vinegar

Preheat oven to 180°C.

Place the carrots in a
baking dish.

Combine the sugar, butter and
vinegar in a small bowl. Pour
over the carrots and toss to coat.

Bake in the oven, tossing
occasionally, for 45 minutes or
until carrots are tender.

Drizzle the glaze over to serve.

BEANS WITH BACON AND GARLIC

Salmon and Cucumber with Dill Mayonnaise Page 47

Halloumi with Chilli Oil and Lime V Page 39

Fresh Goat's Cheese with Raspberry Coulis V Page 39

Prawn, Mango and Spinach Salad Page 297

Mediterranean Chicken Page 153

Roast Duck with Red Wine Sauce Page 157

Lemon and Raspberry Baskets Page 319

Beans with Bacon and Garlic

Serves 4

5 rashers back bacon, chopped
2 cloves garlic, crushed

500g green beans,
cut into 2cm lengths

Place bacon in large frying pan, cook until crisp. Stir in garlic and cook for a further minute.

Add beans to bacon, cook, stirring, for about 8 minutes or until beans are bright green and still slightly firm.

BRAISED RED CABBAGE

Braised Red Cabbage v

Serves 4

450g red cabbage

Quarter, core and thinly shred cabbage and place in large saucepan.

100g Demerara sugar
300ml red wine vinegar

Add sugar and vinegar to the cabbage and bring to the boil over high heat, stirring occasionally. Simmer until the cabbage is tender and the liquid has thickened to a light syrup (if the liquid thickens too much add a splash of water to correct consistency).

Note: This can be allowed to cool and reheated slowly at a later stage.

CAJUN POTATO WEDGES

Cajun Potato Wedges v

Serves 6-8

1.5kg potatoes, scrubbed

4 tbsp olive oil
90g butter, melted
3 tbsp Cajun seasoning
3 tbsp ground cumin

Preheat oven to 200°C.

Halve the unpeeled potatoes and cut each half into 4 wedges. Boil until just tender then cool.

Combine the oil, butter and spices in a large bowl, add the potatoes and mix gently to coat well.

Place the wedges in a single layer in roasting tins and bake for 45 minutes or until crisp.

CHILLI
BROCCOLI

Chilli Broccoli v

Serves 4

2 tbsp oil
2 small red chillies, deseeded
and finely chopped
1 onion, finely chopped
1 clove garlic, crushed

450g broccoli, cut into
very small florets

Heat a wok or large pan and heat the oil. Then add the chillies, onion and garlic. Turn down the heat and cook gently, stirring, until onions are slightly golden.

Add the broccoli and stir fry for about 7 minutes or until cooked to your liking.

COUSCOUS WITH CHERRY TOMATOES

Couscous with Cherry Tomatoes

Serves 6

300g couscous
1 bunch spring onions, thinly sliced

1 tbsp olive oil
450ml hot chicken or vegetable stock

150g cherry tomatoes, quartered

Put couscous in a bowl and add spring onions.

Mix olive oil and hot stock together then pour onto couscous. Stir well then cover with clingfilm and leave for 5-6 minutes or until all the liquid is absorbed.

Fluff up couscous with a fork and stir in tomatoes.

CREAMY SCALLOPED POTATOES

Creamy Scalloped Potatoes v

Serves 4

6 medium potatoes, peeled and sliced into 1cm thick slices

250ml double cream
2 cloves garlic, crushed
125g Cheddar cheese, grated

Preheat oven to 180°C.

Simmer potatoes until they are just tender. Place the sliced potatoes into a shallow dish forming 2-3 layers.

In a small saucepan gently warm the cream and crushed garlic making sure it doesn't boil. Pour the cream and garlic over the layered potatoes and top with the grated cheese.

Bake for approximately 30 minutes or until cooked and golden on top.

GARLIC
COURGETTES

Simply 3 - 5

Garlic Courgettes v

Serves 4

4 courgettes

Top and tail courgettes, cut into ½cm slices.

2 tbsp olive oil
2 shallots, finely diced

Heat oil and add shallots, cook gently for a few minutes.

2 cloves garlic, crushed
1 tbsp chopped flat leaf parsley

Add courgettes and garlic, toss lightly in the hot oil for 1½-2 minutes. Serve sprinkled with the chopped parsley.

GINGER AND ORANGE PUMPKIN

Ginger and Orange Pumpkin v

Serves 4

300g pumpkin, peeled
and thickly sliced
2 tbsp honey
juice of 1 orange
½ tsp finely grated ginger

Preheat oven to 180°C.

Place the pumpkin in an
ovenproof dish. Combine the
honey, orange juice and ginger
and pour over pumpkin.

Bake in oven for 35-45 minutes
or until tender.

GORGONZOLA POTATO PARCELS

Gorgonzola Potato Parcels

Serves 8

1.5kg small new potatoes	Boil the potatoes in a large pan of salted water for about 10 minutes, or until just starting to soften. Drain and cool.
	Cut out 8 x 30cm squares of foil and the same of greaseproof paper. Lay a piece of greaseproof on top of each square of foil then divide the potatoes between them.
8 rashers streaky bacon, chopped, or 100g cubed pancetta 175g Gorgonzola, diced 8 thyme sprigs	Scatter with the bacon or pancetta, Gorgonzola and thyme. Seal together the sides of the foil to make a parcel.
	Put the parcels to one side of the barbecue and cook for 20 minutes or if you prefer cook in the oven at 180°C for about 30 minutes.
	Note: The parcels can be prepared the day before and heated just before serving.

HONEYED SWEET POTATOES

Honeyed Sweet Potatoes v

Serves 6

1kg sweet potatoes, peeled
and halved

25g butter
4 tbsp orange juice
2 tbsp honey

Preheat oven to 200°C.

Lightly grease a shallow baking
dish.

Cook the potatoes in boiling
water until just tender. Drain.
Arrange potatoes in the dish.

Heat together butter, orange
juice and honey. Spoon over the
potatoes and bake for 15-20
minutes until tender.

LEEK MASH

Simply 3 - 5

Leek Mash v

Serves 4

1kg baking potatoes
2 leeks

Boil potatoes in their jackets.
Meanwhile, remove dark green
leaves from top of leeks and
wash and slice remainder of
leek.

50g butter

Heat 25g of the butter in a
saucepan and when foaming add
the sliced leeks. Toss gently to
coat and cover with a lid. Cook
very gently for about 10
minutes, until soft and moist but
not coloured.

150ml milk, approximately
1 tbsp chopped chives

Bring milk and chives to the boil
and leave to infuse.

When potatoes are tender drain
well. Peel while hot and mash
immediately, mix with most of
the milk until it is the
consistency you like. Add
drained leeks and beat in the
last 25g of the butter.
Gently reheat, stirring over low
heat.

Note: This is great because it
can be made ahead and reheated
later in oven at 180°C. Just
make sure you cover the dish
with foil or a lid to prevent a
skin forming.

LEMON BUTTER SPINACH

Lemon Butter Spinach v

Serves 4

60g butter
1 tbsp finely grated lemon rind
2 cloves garlic, crushed

Place the butter in a saucepan over high heat. Add the lemon rind and garlic and cook for 1 minute or until the garlic is lightly golden.

400g baby spinach leaves
2 tbsp lemon juice

Add the spinach and turn with tongs until soft and wilted. Pour over the lemon juice. Serve immediately.

MEDITERRANEAN RICE

Simply 3 - 5

Mediterranean Rice v

Serves 4

300g brown rice

Cook the rice in boiling water until tender then drain well.

2 tbsp olive oil
150g black olives
150g semidried tomatoes
zest and juice of 1 small lemon

Heat the olive oil in a frying pan and add the olives, semidried tomatoes and lemon zest. Cook gently for 2 minutes. Pour in the lemon juice and cook for a further 2 minutes.

40g pine nuts

Add the rice and pine nuts and heat through, gently stirring.

MINT AND BUTTER PEAS

Mint and Butter Peas

Serves 4

400g frozen peas
150ml chicken or vegetable stock
40g butter

2 tbsp chopped mint leaves
2 tbsp grated Parmesan cheese

Place the peas and stock in a saucepan over medium heat and cook, covered, for 5 minutes or until the peas are soft. Remove from the heat, drain and roughly mash with the butter.

Stir in the mint and Parmesan and serve.

MOROCCAN COUSCOUS

Moroccan Couscous v

Serves 6

2 courgettes, diced
2 red peppers, diced

2 tbsp Ras El Hanout
375ml boiling water
275g couscous
2 tbsp chopped coriander leaves

Lightly steam or gently fry the courgette and pepper until still crisp.

Mix the Ras El Hanout and water into the couscous. Cover and leave to swell for about 5 minutes. Fluff up with a fork and mix in the vegetables and coriander.

PILAFF RICE

Simply 3 - 5

Pilaff Rice

Serves 4

50g butter
25g chopped onion
250g basmati rice

600ml chicken or vegetable stock

Preheat oven to 180°C.

Place half the butter in an ovenproof pan and add onion. Cook gently without colouring for 2-3 minutes. Add the rice.

Add the stock and cover with a piece of buttered baking paper. Bring to the boil.

Place in oven for about 15 minutes or until rice is cooked, carefully mix in the remaining butter.

Note: Just press the buttered paper down on to the rice. It stops the top of the rice drying out.

ROAST PUMPKIN AND POTATO WITH GARLIC AND ROSEMARY

Simply 3 - 5

Roast Pumpkin and Potato with Garlic and Rosemary v

Serves 4

750g butternut pumpkin,
chopped into chunks
750g medium potatoes,
chopped into chunks
1 tbsp olive oil
2 cloves garlic, sliced thinly

2 tbsp fresh rosemary leaves,
very finely chopped

Preheat oven to 190°C.

Combine pumpkin, potato, oil
and garlic in large roasting tin.
Roast, uncovered, for about 1
hour or until vegetables are just
tender and browned lightly.

Sprinkle with rosemary and
serve.

ROASTED BABY VEGETABLES

Roasted Baby Vegetables v

Serves 6

2 tbsp olive oil
500g baby onions, peeled
1kg tiny new potatoes, unpeeled

6 baby aubergines,
halved lengthways
250g cherry tomatoes

Preheat oven to 190°C.

Heat oil in a roasting tin for a few minutes, then add onions and potatoes. Stir to coat vegetables in the oil then roast for 20-25 minutes or until the potatoes are almost tender.

Add aubergine and tomatoes and roast for a further 10 minutes.

ROASTED CARAMELISED PARSNIPS

Roasted Caramelised Parsnips v

Serves 6

kg parsnips, halved lengthways
tbsp olive oil
tbsp brown sugar
tsp ground nutmeg

Preheat oven to 200°C.

Combine the parsnips, oil, sugar and nutmeg in a large baking dish. Roast, turning occasionally for 50 minutes or until parsnips are browned and tender.

ROASTED MUSHROOMS

Simply 3 - 5

Roasted Mushrooms v

Serves 6

500g button mushrooms
500g chestnut mushrooms
3 cloves garlic, crushed
2 tbsp olive oil

Preheat oven to 200°C.

Combine ingredients in a large bowl. Place mixture in a single layer in a baking dish. Roast for about 20 minutes or until mushrooms are soft and lightly browned.

SOY RICE

Soy Rice v

Serves 4

225g basmati rice
500ml hot water

Place the rice in a microwave safe bowl along with the hot water and cook on High for 3 minutes then on Medium for 12 minutes.

125ml soy sauce
tbsp brown sugar
tbsp grated ginger

A few minutes before the rice is cooked place the soy sauce, sugar and ginger in a saucepan over a high heat. Bring to the boil and boil for 1 minute. To serve, place the rice into serving bowls and spoon over soy mixture.

Note: You can cook the rice, according to the packet instructions, on the stovetop if preferred.

SALADS

Simply 3 - 5

Salads

Asparagus, Pear and Baby Beetroot Salad V   291
Serves 6

Chickpea and Tomato Salad V   291
Serves 4

Citrus Coleslaw V   293
Serves 4

Courgette and Pine Nut Salad V   293
Serves 4

Cucumber, Tomato and Chilli Salad V   293
Serves 6

Mango and Avocado Salad V   295
Serves 4

Melon, Halloumi and Coriander Salad V   295
Serves 4

Mixed Bean Salad V   295
Serves 4

Orange and Watercress Salad V   297
Serves 2

SALADS

Simply 3 - 5

Salads

Prawn, Mango and Spinach Salad   297
Serves 4

Prosciutto with Melon and Rocket   299
Serves 2

Pumpkin and Halloumi Salad V   301
Serves 4

Simple Pasta Salad V   301
Serves 4

Warm Potato Salad with Sweet Chilli Cream V   303
Serves 4

Wild Rice and Spinach Salad V   303
Serves 6

ASPARAGUS, PEAR AND BABY BEETROOT SALAD

CHICKPEA AND TOMATO SALAD

Asparagus, Pear and Baby Beetroot Salad v

Serves 6

2 bunches asparagus, trimmed

Bring a saucepan of water to the boil and add the asparagus. Simmer for 2-3 minutes until just tender. Drain and rinse under cold water. Slice in half lengthways.

2 small pears, skin on and sliced thinly
1 jar baby beetroot, drained
100g rocket
50g Parmesan cheese, shaved

Toss together asparagus, pears, beetroot and rocket leaves. Arrange on a platter and top with Parmesan cheese.

Chickpea and Tomato Salad v

Serves 4

1 x 400g can chickpeas
1 tomato, chopped
½ small red onion, finely chopped
1 tbsp olive oil
2 tbsp balsamic vinegar

Drain the chickpeas and place in a bowl with all the remaining ingredients. Toss to combine.

CITRUS COLESLAW

COURGETTE AND PINE NUT SALAD

CUCUMBER, TOMATO AND CHILLI SALAD

Simply 3 - 5

Citrus Coleslaw v

Serves 4

1 orange
180g white cabbage, shredded
2 spring onions, sliced
1 small green pepper, seeded and
sliced
2 tbsp mayonnaise

Peel and slice the orange into segments or rings. Place the orange with the cabbage, spring onions and pepper in a bowl. Add the mayonnaise and mix well.

Courgette and Pine Nut Salad v

Serves 4

4 courgettes, sliced lengthways,
with a mandoline or vegetable
peeler
4 tbsp toasted pine nuts
handful of basil leaves, torn
Parmesan shavings
2 tbsp salad dressing

Put all these ingredients in a bowl and mix well together.

Cucumber, Tomato and Chilli Salad v

Serves 6

1 cucumber, peeled
250g cherry tomatoes
2 shallots, finely sliced
2 small chillies, finely diced
1 tbsp cider or rice wine vinegar

Finely slice the cucumber and halve the cherry tomatoes. Toss these with the shallots and chillies, and dress with the vinegar.

MANGO AND AVOCADO SALAD

MELON, HALLOUMI AND CORIANDER SALAD

MIXED BEAN SALAD

Simply 3 - 5

Mango and Avocado Salad v

Serves 4

1 mango, peeled and chopped
1 large avocado, chopped
1 small red onion, chopped finely
1 small red pepper, chopped finely
2 tbsp lime juice

Gently combine all ingredients in a bowl.

Melon, Halloumi and Coriander Salad v

Serves 4

1 lemon, zest and juice
4 tbsp olive oil

Whisk together and set aside.

250g halloumi cheese, diced and grilled
1 honeydew melon, peeled and cubed
4 large handful's coriander leaves

Put all these ingredients into a bowl. Toss with the dressing and serve immediately.

Mixed Bean Salad v

Serves 4

75g baby green beans, topped and tailed

Cook the green beans until just tender. Plunge the beans into very cold water to retain their green colour. Cut beans into bite size pieces.

1 x 400g can mixed beans
1 clove garlic, crushed
1 tbsp lemon juice
1 tbsp olive oil

Drain and rinse the bean mix and place in a bowl with the green beans, garlic, lemon juice and oil. Toss to combine.

Note: If you really like garlic you can use 2 cloves in this recipe.

ORANGE AND WATERCRESS SALAD

PRAWN, MANGO AND SPINACH SALAD

Simply 3 - 5

Orange and Watercress Salad v

Serves 2

1 orange, peeled and divided into segments
1 bag watercress
2 tbsp olive oil
2 tsp fresh orange juice

Arrange the orange segments on a bed of the watercress. Whisk together the oil and orange juice and pour over the salad.

Prawn, Mango and Spinach Salad

Serves 4

125g baby spinach leaves
200g cooked and peeled tiger prawns
1 large mango, peeled and sliced
2 tbsp salad dressing
2 spring onions, sliced thinly

Lay the spinach in a bowl and top with the prawns and mango. Pour over the dressing and gently toss together. Sprinkle the spring onion over the top.

PROSCIUTTO WITH MELON AND ROCKET

Prosciutto with Melon and Rocket

Serves 2

1 small ripe melon	Cut the melon in half and scoop out the seeds. Use a melon baller or teaspoon to scoop out bite sized pieces of melon. Put the pieces in a bowl with the melon juices.
75g rocket leaves	Add the rocket leaves to the bowl.
75g prosciutto 1 tbsp white wine vinegar 3 tbsp extra virgin olive oil	Cut the prosciutto into smaller pieces and add to the melon and rocket. Mix the vinegar and oil and pour over salad. Toss carefully and serve.

PUMPKIN AND HALLOUMI SALAD

SIMPLE PASTA SALAD

Simply 3 - 5

Pumpkin and Halloumi Salad v

Serves 4

Preheat oven to 180°C.

400g pumpkin, peeled and
cut into 2cm pieces

Place pumpkin in a lightly oiled
roasting tin and bake for about
15 minutes or until tender.
Allow to cool.

125g halloumi cheese,
cut into 1 x 2cm pieces

Fry the halloumi, turning once,
until golden on both sides.

75g baby spinach leaves
50g walnuts
2 tbsp French dressing

In a bowl combine the spinach
leaves, pumpkin, halloumi,
walnuts and dressing.

Simple Pasta Salad v

Serves 4

125g penne pasta

Cook the pasta until just tender.
Drain and set aside to cool.

1 small red pepper
1 small green pepper
½ small red onion, chopped
1-2 tbsp mayonnaise

Slice the red and green pepper
into thin strips and add to the
pasta with the onion and
mayonnaise. Mix well to
combine.

WARM POTATO SALAD WITH SWEET CHILLI CREAM

WILD RICE AND SPINACH SALAD

Simply 3 - 5

Warm Potato Salad with Sweet Chilli Cream v

Serves 4

Preheat oven to 180°C.

1kg salad potatoes, rinsed and halved
2 tbsp olive oil

Place the potatoes in a single layer in a large roasting tin. Drizzle with olive oil and toss to coat. Roast for 40-50 minutes, turning once, until golden and tender. Allow to cool for 5 minutes.

190ml sour cream
2 tbsp sweet chilli sauce
2 spring onions, chopped

Place potatoes in a large bowl. Combine sour cream, chilli sauce and spring onions. Pour over the potato and toss to coat.

Wild Rice and Spinach Salad v

Serves 6

300g basmati and wild rice
80g pine nuts, toasted
80g baby spinach leaves
2 spring onions, sliced thinly
3-4 tbsp salad dressing

Cook the rice until tender, drain and cool slightly. In a bowl combine the rice, pine nuts, spinach leaves and onions. Toss with the dressing.

DESSERTS

Simply 3 - 5

Desserts

DESSERTS

Simply 3 - 5

Desserts

CARAMEL ORANGES

Simply 3 - 5

Caramel Oranges

Serves 4

6 large, juicy oranges

Peel one of the oranges carefully, leaving the pith behind. Cut peel into thin shreds and set aside. Peel the other oranges and segment all 6 oranges.

Arrange the oranges in a bowl.

300ml of water

Bring the water to the boil, add the shreds of orange peel and simmer for 5 minutes. Strain the water and reserve the peel.

100g granulated sugar
1 tbsp water

Dissolve the sugar in 1 tablespoon of water over a low heat then cook until just beginning to turn golden. Return the peel to the pan and pour in 250ml cold water very carefully as it is likely to splutter. Remove the pan from the heat and stir until the caramel and water are blended.

1 cinnamon stick

Allow the sauce to cool for 1 minute, add the cinnamon stick and pour it over the oranges. Chill for 2 hours or preferably overnight to allow the flavours to develop. Remove the cinnamon stick from the sauce and serve.

CHOCOLATE MOUSSE

Chocolate Mousse

Serves 4

120g dark chocolate, broken up
4 eggs, separated

Place chocolate in a bowl over a saucepan of gently simmering water. Heat gently, stirring, until melted. Remove from the heat and allow to cool slightly.
Blend in the egg yolks.

300ml double cream

Whip cream until thick.
Fold into chocolate mixture.

In a separate bowl, beat egg whites until stiff peaks form. Fold gently into the chocolate cream mixture. Pour into serving dishes and refrigerate for several hours.

COOKIES AND VANILLA ICE CREAM

Simply 3 - 5

Cookies and Vanilla Ice Cream

Serves 4

500ml cream
395g can condensed milk
1 tsp vanilla essence
150g chocolate cookies,
roughly crumbled

Beat cream, condensed milk and
vanilla essence in a bowl with
an electric whisk until thick
and creamy. Fold in the biscuit
pieces.

Pour mixture into a suitable
container. Cover and freeze.

FUDGE CHEESECAKE

Fudge Cheesecake

Serves 10

250g hob nobs, crushed
75g butter, melted

200g cream cheese
300g fudge
600ml double cream, lightly
whipped

Lightly butter a 24cm springform cake tin.

Combine the biscuits and butter and press into the base of the tin.

Beat the cheese until soft. Melt 150g of the fudge in 125ml of the cream over a low heat for 7-10 minutes. Leave to cool while you whip the remaining cream. Fold the cream into the cheese then fold in the combined melted cream and fudge.

Chop the remaining fudge and scatter over the biscuit base.

Spoon the cream mixture over the top and cover. Chill for between 5-24 hours. Take out of tin carefully and serve in slices.

ICED BERRIES WITH HOT WHITE CHOCOLATE SAUCE

Iced Berries with Hot White Chocolate Sauce

Serves 6

225g white chocolate buttons or grated white chocolate
275ml double cream

500g berries, frozen

Place the chocolate and cream in a bowl over a pan of simmering water for 20-30 minutes, stirring occasionally.

Divide berries between 6 glasses or dessert plates and leave at room temperature for 10-15 minutes.

Transfer chocolate sauce into a serving jug. Allow guests to pour hot sauce over berries at the table.

Note: You can use frozen raspberries or mixed frozen berries.

LEMON AND RASPBERRY BASKETS

Lemon and Raspberry Baskets

Serves 6

50g dark chocolate, broken into pieces

Melt the chocolate in the microwave for 2 minutes on High, stirring halfway through.

200g good quality lemon curd
250g mascarpone
150g fresh raspberries
6 brandy snap baskets

Stir together the lemon curd and the mascarpone. Divide half the raspberries between the baskets, spoon over the lemon cream and top with the rest of the berries.

Drizzle the dark chocolate over the top of the baskets and leave in the fridge to set for 5-10 minutes. Serve immediately or the baskets will go soft.

ORANGE AND BASIL SORBET

Orange and Basil Sorbet

Serves 4

250g caster sugar
250ml water

Gently heat the sugar with the water until dissolved, then simmer for 2 minutes.

a large bunch of basil
4 oranges, juice and zest

Tear the basil leaves, add to the syrup and infuse until cool. Strain, mix with the orange juice and zest then churn in an ice cream maker until frozen, or freeze in a container stirring once or twice until frozen.

PAIN AU CHOCOLAT PUDDING

Pain Au Chocolat Pudding

Serves 4

4 pain au chocolat

4 eggs
150ml milk
150ml cream
60g sugar

Preheat oven to 160°C.

Slice the pain au chocolat and layer into a buttered ovenproof dish.

Whisk the eggs, milk, cream and sugar together and pour over the pain au chocolat. Bake uncovered for 35 minutes or until risen and browned.

Note: You can bake this in advance and just reheat for 10-15 minutes.

PAVLOVA

Simply 3 - 5

Pavlova

Serves 6

Preheat oven to 120°C.

Cover a greased oven tray with baking paper.

4 egg whites

Place egg whites in bowl and beat with an electric whisk on high speed for about 1 minute or until soft peaks form.

225g caster sugar

Gradually add sugar, 1 tablespoon at a time, beating well after each addition, until sugar dissolves.

Spoon meringue into a round shape approximately 20cm in diameter on the prepared oven tray. Level top of meringue gently with a rubber spatula.

Bake in oven for about 1½ hours or until meringue feels firm and dry to the touch. Turn oven off, open oven door and leave meringue to cool slowly in oven.

300ml double cream

Beat cream with an electric mixer on medium speed until soft peaks form.

500g raspberries or strawberries

Turn meringue onto serving platter and top with cream and fruit.

PINK CHAMPAGNE JELLY

Pink Champagne Jelly

Serves 6

8 gelatine leaves

Place the gelatine in a large bowl and cover with cold water. Leave aside for 5 minutes or until soft.

250ml water
125g caster sugar

Put the water and the sugar in a saucepan and bring to the boil, stirring to melt the sugar. Turn off the heat. Drain the gelatine, add to the syrup in the pan and stir to dissolve completely. Pour into a large bowl and leave until cold and starting to go syrupy.

1 bottle pink Champagne or Cava
raspberries, to decorate

Stir the Champagne or Cava gently into the sugar and water mixture, allowing the bubbles to subside, then pour into glasses to within 1cm of the top, cover and refrigerate for several hours until set. Put 3 raspberries on top of each and serve.

Note: This works well with Cava or Champagne. It is a refreshing dessert after a big meal.

RHUBARB GALETTE

Rhubarb Galette

Serves 4

Preheat oven to 200°C.

Line a baking tray with baking paper.

30g butter, melted
300g coarsely chopped rhubarb
75g brown sugar

Combine 20g of the butter with the rhubarb and sugar in a bowl.

1 sheet ready rolled puff pastry
3 tbsp ground almonds

Cut a 25cm round from the pastry, place on oven tray and sprinkle almonds evenly over pastry. Spread rhubarb mixture over pastry, leaving a 4cm edge. Fold 2cm of the pastry edge up and around filling and brush the edge with the leftover butter.

Bake galette for about 20 minutes or until lightly browned.

ROAST STRAWBERRIES

Simply 3 - 5

Roast Strawberries

Serves 4

Preheat oven to 200°C.

Line a shallow baking dish with baking paper.

750g strawberries, hulled
and sliced
1 tbsp sugar

Place strawberries into the dish and sprinkle with the sugar. Roast for 20 minutes or until strawberries are tender. Set aside to cool for 15 minutes.

180ml Greek style yoghurt
1 tsp ground cinnamon

Combine the yoghurt and cinnamon and spoon into 4 dishes. Top with the strawberries and drizzle with the pan juices.

SHORTCAKE APPLE CRUMBLE

Shortcake Apple Crumble

Serves 4

Preheat oven to 180°C.

Lightly grease an ovenproof, microwave safe dish.

6 medium Granny Smith apples, peeled, cored and thinly sliced

Layer the apple in the dish. Cover with clingfilm and microwave for 5 minutes on High or until apples are just tender.

125g butter
90g brown sugar
250g shortcake biscuits, crushed
1 tsp cinnamon

Meanwhile, cream the butter and sugar until mixture is light and fluffy. Mix in the crushed biscuits and cinnamon and spread the crumb mixture evenly over the top of the apples.

Bake in the oven for 30 minutes or until topping is golden and apples are tender.

Note: To crush biscuits, place in a plastic bag and bash with a rolling pin.

STRAWBERRY LAYERED CHEESECAKE

Strawberry Layered Cheesecake

Serves 8

250g cream cheese, at room temperature
300ml sour cream
2 large oranges, juiced and rind finely grated

250g packet sponge fingers
500g strawberries,
hulled and sliced

Lightly grease a 20 x 8 x 7cm deep loaf pan with baking paper.

Whisk the cream cheese in a bowl until smooth. Add sour cream and orange rind and stir well until combined and smooth.

Place the orange juice in a bowl. Dip 6 sponge fingers into the orange juice one at a time and line the base of the pan, trimming fingers if necessary. Spoon one third of the cream cheese mixture over the biscuits and top with a layer of strawberries. Repeat twice more ending with the cream cheese mixture. Refrigerate for at least 2-3 hours or until set.

Transfer to a serving platter and top with remaining strawberries.

WHITE CHOCOLATE TORTE

White Chocolate Torte

Serves 8

50g butter 200g amaretti biscuits, finely crushed in a food processor	Melt the butter in a saucepan, add the biscuits and mix well. Butter an 18cm loose based round tin and press the biscuits into the base using the back of a spoon or your hands. Freeze until cold.
300g white chocolate, chopped	Melt the chocolate in a bowl set over a pan of simmering water. Once melted leave to cool.
400ml double cream	Whisk the cream until you can leave a ribbon like trail for a couple of seconds. If your cream is very cold then leave it to come to room temperature otherwise it won't mix with the chocolate. Add 3 tablespoons of the whipped cream to the chocolate and stir it in. Pour the chocolate mix into the remaining cream and mix well. Pour into the tin and chill until firm. Note: You can either buy amaretti biscuits or use the recipe in the biscuit section to make your own.

SAUCES

Simply 3 - 5

Sauces

Savoury Sauces

Red Wine Sauce   341
Serves 4

Satay Sauce V   341
Makes 250ml

Tartare Sauce V   343
Makes 250ml

Teriyaki Stir Fry Sauce   343
Serves 4

Sweet Sauces

Chantilly Cream   345
Serves 4

Hot Chocolate Fudge Sauce   345
Serves 4-6

Pecan Toffee Sauce   347
Serves 4

Quick and Easy Custard   349
Makes 500ml

Vanilla Raspberry Sauce   349
Makes about 375ml

RED WINE SAUCE

SATAY SAUCE

Red Wine Sauce

Serves 4

50g butter
120ml red wine
250ml beef stock
2 tbsp redcurrant jelly

Place all the ingredients in a small saucepan and simmer for 8-10 minutes.

Satay Sauce v

Makes 250ml

½ small onion, finely chopped

Place the onion in a small saucepan and using a little water cook the onion gently until it is soft and translucent.

120g crunchy peanut butter
2 tbsp soy sauce
2 tbsp sweet chilli sauce
125ml coconut cream

Add the remaining ingredients to the pan and stir until well combined. Continue to stir for a couple of minutes until heated through and ready to serve.

Note: If you want a hotter sauce just add more sweet chilli sauce.

Rice Wine Sauce

TARTARE SAUCE

TERIYAKI STIR FRY SAUCE

Simply 3 - 5

Tartare Sauce v

Makes 250ml

250ml mayonnaise
1 gherkin, finely chopped
2 tsp capers, finely chopped
1 tbsp flat leaf parsley, chopped
juice of ½ small lemon plus ½ tsp
grated lemon zest

Place all ingredients in a small
bowl and mix to combine.

Note: This sauce goes well with
the Calamari in the Fish section.

Teriyaki Stir Fry Sauce

Serves 4

75ml teriyaki marinade
45ml soy sauce
30ml Worcestershire sauce
1 clove garlic, crushed
1 tsp grated ginger

Mix all ingredients together.

Note: This is great for chicken
or beef stir fries.

CHANTILLY CREAM

HOT CHOCOLATE FUDGE SAUCE

Simply 3 - 5

Chantilly Cream

Serves 4

250ml double cream
30g icing sugar
¼ tsp vanilla extract

Whip cream and icing sugar together until cream stands in soft peaks. Flavour with vanilla.

Note: A true Chantilly wouldn't have vanilla in it. This is a lovely way to serve cream. Use instead of plain whipped cream.

Hot Chocolate Fudge Sauce

Serves 4-6

395g can condensed milk
200g dark chocolate, roughly chopped
1 tbsp butter

Place condensed milk, chocolate and butter into a microwave safe jug. Melt on Medium for 2 minutes, stirring halfway through cooking. Mix well to combine.

1 tbsp double cream

Add the cream and stir through.

Note: This can be made ahead of time and when ready to serve reheat in the microwave on Medium for 1 minute.

PECAN TOFFEE SAUCE

Simply 3 - 5

Pecan Toffee Sauce

Serves 4

50g caster sugar
50g pecan nuts, chopped
150ml double cream

Place sugar in a pan and cook, swirling the pan over a low heat until dissolved and a caramel has formed. Add the pecan nuts, shaking the pan until the nuts are well coated in the caramel. Pour in the cream and cook gently, stirring until evenly mixed and slightly thickened.

Note: Don't stir until you add the cream otherwise the sugar will crystallise, just swirl the pan.

QUICK AND EASY CUSTARD

VANILLA RASPBERRY SAUCE

Simply 3 - 5

Quick and Easy Custard

Makes 500ml

50g caster sugar
2 egg yolks
1 tsp cornflour

375ml milk
½ tsp vanilla essence

Combine the sugar, egg yolks and cornflour in a bowl. Whisk for a minute or two until thick and creamy.

Slowly whisk milk into the egg yolk mixture. Pour into a saucepan. Cook, whisking, over a low to medium heat until the custard thickens (about 5-7 minutes). Don't allow the custard to boil.

Stir in the vanilla essence.

Note: This custard can be served warm or cold. On cooling the custard becomes quite thick, extra milk can be added, if necessary, to achieve the desired consistency.

Vanilla Raspberry Sauce

Makes about 375ml

200g frozen raspberries
2½ tbsp caster sugar
1½ tsp vanilla essence

Place all ingredients in a small saucepan over a medium heat. Cook, stirring occasionally until the sugar has dissolved and the berries have broken down. The syrup will thicken slightly whilst cooking.

349

DRESSINGS, MARINADES AND RUBS

Simply 3 - 5
Dressings, Marinades and Rubs

Dressings

Marinades

Rubs

AVOCADO DRESSING

Avocado Dressing v

Makes about 250ml

1 avocado
80ml Greek style yoghurt
squeeze of lemon juice

Mash the avocado with the yoghurt until blended and smooth. Add the lemon juice to taste. Cover and chill until required.

Note: This needs to be made no more than a few hours before serving as it will discolour. This goes well with a spinach salad and also seafood.

BASIC VINAIGRETTE

Basic Vinaigrette

(This will dress a small salad)

1 tbsp white wine vinegar	Place in a small bowl.
pinch salt pinch ground black pepper	Add to vinegar and mix well to dissolve salt.
3 tbsp olive oil	Add to bowl and beat well to mix and thicken.

Variations
Just stir any of the following into the basic recipe.

1 tbsp chopped chives, gherkins or capers
2 tsp grated horseradish
2 tsp Worcestershire sauce
A few drops of chilli sauce
1 tbsp crumbled Danish Blue, Roquefort or Stilton
A little chopped garlic
2 tsp fresh chopped herbs

Note: Will keep for about 5 days in a cool place. Don't add fresh herbs until just prior to serving.

CHILLI LIME DRESSING

HERB MAYONNAISE

MAYONNAISE

Simply 3 - 5

Chilli Lime Dressing v

Serves 4

½ fresh long red chilli, sliced thinly
1 tsp finely grated lime rind, plus 5 tbsp lime juice
1 clove garlic, crushed
2 tsp finely chopped coriander leaves
2 tbsp olive oil

Place all ingredients in a jar and shake.

Note: This is lovely and goes well with fish or chicken.

Herb Mayonnaise v

Makes about 125ml

125ml mayonnaise
2 tbsp finely chopped basil
2 tbsp finely chopped flat leaf parsley

Combine the mayonnaise with the herbs and mix well.

Note: This goes well on a potato salad, pasta salad or plain green salad.

Mayonnaise v

Makes about 300ml

2 large egg yolks
½ tsp French or English mustard
1 tbsp vinegar or lemon juice
250ml olive oil or half olive, half sunflower oil

Beat egg yolks until thick and creamy. Add mustard and vinegar or lemon juice and, using a hand whisk, whisk for 30 seconds. Add a drop of oil and whisk until incorporated. Keep whisking and adding a drop of oil at a time. When the mixture is thick add oil in a steady trickle.

357

RED WINE VINEGAR DRESSING

THOUSAND ISLAND DRESSING

BARBECUE, HONEY AND SWEET CHILLI MARINADE

Simply 3 - 5

Red Wine Vinegar Dressing v

Makes 250ml

80ml red wine vinegar
160ml olive oil
1 clove garlic, crushed
½ tsp Dijon mustard

Mix all ingredients together.

Thousand Island Dressing

Makes 175ml

125ml mayonnaise
2 tbsp tomato paste
2 tbsp tomato ketchup
1 tsp Worcestershire sauce
¼ tsp Tabasco sauce

Combine all ingredients in a small bowl. Whisk until ingredients are smooth and well blended.

Note: Can be used in salads, burgers, sandwiches or with seafood.

Barbecue, Honey and Sweet Chilli Marinade v

Serves 4-6

8 tbsp barbecue sauce
6 tbsp sweet chilli sauce
2 tbsp honey
1 tbsp oil

Mix all ingredients together.

Note: This marinade is great with beef or lamb. Marinade for 4 hours or preferably overnight.

HONEY, GARLIC AND SOY MARINADE

LIME AND WASABI MARINADE

TANDOORI MARINADE

Simply 3 - 5

Honey, Garlic and Soy Marinade v

Serves 4

2½ tbsp soy sauce
1 tbsp sesame oil
1 tbsp lemon juice
1 tbsp honey
1 clove garlic, crushed

Mix all ingredients together.

Note: This marinade is great with chicken, pork or lamb. Marinade for a minimum of 1 hour.

Lime and Wasabi Marinade v

Serves 4

4 tbsp lime juice
2½ tbsp vegetable oil
1 tsp wasabi paste
¼ tsp sesame oil

Mix all ingredients together.

Note: This marinade is great with chicken. Marinade for 2 hours or overnight. Add more wasabi paste if you want it hotter.

Tandoori Marinade

Serves 4

4 tbsp tandoori paste
1 tsp ground cumin
1 tbsp lemon juice
250ml natural yoghurt
1 clove garlic, crushed

Mix all ingredients together.

Note: This marinade is great with chicken. Marinade for 30 minutes or overnight.

361

BASIL SPICE RUB

CHILLI SPICE RUB

MOROCCAN SPICE RUB

Simply 3 - 5

Basil Spice Rub v

Serves 4

1 tsp garlic salt
½ tsp pepper
a few fresh basil leaves, finely chopped
¼ tsp cayenne pepper

Mix all ingredients together. Rub mixture onto meat 30 minutes prior to cooking.

Note: This rub is good with chicken and pork.

Chilli Spice Rub v

Serves 4-6

1½ tsp chilli powder
½ tsp ground cumin
½ tsp garlic salt
¼ tsp cayenne pepper

Mix all ingredients together. Rub mixture onto meat 30 minutes prior to cooking.

Note: This rub is very spicy and great for beef.

Moroccan Spice Rub v

Serves 4

1 tsp ground cumin
1 tsp cinnamon
1 tsp sweet paprika
½ tsp turmeric
pinch cayenne

Mix all ingredients together. Rub mixture onto meat 30 minutes prior to cooking.

Note: This rub can be used on chicken, fish or any meat.

CAKES AND SCONES

Simply 3 - 5

Cakes and Scones

APRICOT AND COCONUT LOAF

Apricot and Coconut Loaf

Cuts into 10 slices

Preheat oven to 180°C.

Butter and flour a 900g loaf tin.

150g self raising flour
125g white sugar
85g desiccated coconut
180g dried apricots, diced
250ml milk

Combine the flour, sugar, coconut and apricots then add the milk. Mix well with a wooden spoon. Pour into the tin and bake for 40-50 minutes.

BLUEBERRY SCONES

Blueberry Scones

Makes about 20 scones

1kg self raising flour
225g butter, softened

150g sugar
350g blueberries
450ml milk, plus a little extra for brushing tops

Preheat oven to 200°C.

Grease a large baking sheet.

Sift the flour into a large mixing bowl. Add the butter and rub in with your fingers until the mixture resembles fine breadcrumbs.

Add the sugar, blueberries and milk then mix together until you have a soft dough.

Turn the dough out onto a floured board and roll to a thickness of 2cm. Using a 5cm cutter, cut out as many scones as you can.

Place the scones on the baking sheet and lightly brush tops with the extra milk. Bake for 20-25 minutes or until lightly browned and firm to the touch. Can be served lukewam or cold.

BLUE CHEESE SCONES

Blue Cheese Scones

Makes 12 small scones

150g self raising flour
20g butter, chilled and finely chopped

160ml milk
60g blue vein cheese, finely chopped

extra flour, to dust
extra milk, to brush

Preheat oven to 180°C.

Line a baking sheet with baking paper.

Sift the flour into a bowl. Using your fingertips, rub the butter into the flour mixture until it resembles fine breadcrumbs.

Add the milk and cheese. Mix until the dough is just combined and holding together. The dough should be soft but not sticky.

Turn onto a lightly floured surface and very gently knead until smooth. Roll out the dough until 2cm thick then use a 3.5cm round cutter to cut out 12 scones.

Place scones on the baking sheet. Brush the tops with milk and bake for 15 minutes or until golden brown and hollow sounding when tapped.

CHOCOLATE CAKE

Chocolate Cake

Makes 24 squares

Preheat oven to 180°C.

Lightly grease and flour an 18 x 28cm tin.

350g self raising flour
60g cocoa
340g caster sugar
150g butter, softened
250ml water
3 eggs

Sift flour and cocoa into a large bowl and mix in the sugar. Add the butter and combined water and eggs. Use a wooden spoon to combine well. Pour mixture into the tin.

Bake for 40-45 minutes. Allow to cool in the tin for 5 minutes then turn onto a wire rack to cool completely. Cut into squares.

Note: The Chocolate Icing in the Extras Section goes well with this cake

DATE LOAF

Date Loaf

Cuts into 10 slices

Preheat oven to 180°C.

Lightly grease a 900g loaf tin.

225g pitted dates, chopped
110g sugar
40g butter
250ml water

Place dates, sugar, butter and water in a saucepan. Bring to the boil, reduce heat and simmer for 2 minutes. Remove from the heat and cool.

1 egg, lightly beaten
150g self raising flour

Add the egg and mix well. Stir through the sifted flour and pour into the loaf tin.

Bake for 25-30 minutes or until cooked through.

EASY ORANGE CAKE

Simply 3 - 5

Easy Orange Cake

Cuts into 8 slices

whole orange, including skin

eggs
60ml vegetable oil
25g caster sugar
25g self raising flour

Preheat oven to 180°C.

Roughly chop the orange and remove any pips. Place in a food processor and process until the orange is pureed.

Add the eggs, oil and sugar to the processor and process for 30 seconds. Add flour and process until just mixed.

Pour into a 20cm round cake tin and bake for about 35 minutes or until cooked.

Note: The Orange Icing in the Extras Section goes well with this cake.

FLOURLESS MANDARIN CAKE

Flourless Mandarin Cake

Cuts into 6-8 slices

Preheat oven to 180°C.

Lightly grease and line a shallow round 22cm sandwich tin with baking paper.

3 large mandarins
180ml water

Wash the mandarins and slice across the middle, remove the pips. Place the mandarins cut side up in a microwave dish. Pour the water over and cover with a lid. Microwave on High for 15 minutes.

220g sugar

Drain mandarins and place in a food processor with the sugar and process to a paste. Allow to cool.

4 eggs
200g ground almonds
1 tsp baking powder

Add the eggs and process until mixed. Add the almonds and baking powder and process again to mix.

Pour into the cake tin and bake for about 40 minutes. Allow to cool in the tin.

FRUIT CAKE

Simply 3 - 5

Fruit Cake

Cuts into 10 slices

Preheat oven to 180°C.

Line the base of an 18cm round cake tin with baking paper. Butter thoroughly and set aside.

200g butter
150g light soft brown sugar
5 eggs, separated

Using an electric whisk beat the butter and sugar until light and fluffy. Beat the egg yolks into the butter mixture, one at a time until well blended.

200g plain flour
100g mixed fruit

Mix the flour and fruit together and stir gently but thoroughly into the mixture.

Clean the whisk well and beat the egg whites until they form soft peaks. Fold about one third of the beaten whites into the batter. Then carefully fold in the remaining egg whites.

Spoon the batter into the prepared tin and bake in the oven for about 55 minutes.

ITALIAN HAZELNUT CAKE

Italian Hazelnut Cake

Cuts into 10 slices

Preheat oven to 160°C.

Butter and line the base of a 20cm deep, round cake tin.

200g blanched hazelnuts

Grind the hazelnuts in a food processor until they are as fine as you can get them.

5 eggs, separated
175g caster sugar

Put the egg yolks and sugar in a bowl and whisk for about 3 minutes until the mixture leaves a trail on the surface when the blades are lifted.

100g butter, melted
1 tsp vanilla extract

Gradually whisk in the butter then fold in the hazelnuts and vanilla.

Whisk the egg whites until stiff then fold into the cake mixture in four equal batches using the whisk blades.

Pour into the cake tin and bake for 50 minutes or until the cake feels firm and bounces back when pressed in the centre. Leave in the tin for 10 minutes then turn out and peel off the paper. Cool completely.

LEMON DRIZZLE CAKE

Lemon Drizzle Cake

Cuts into 10 slices

Preheat oven to 170°C.

Butter and flour a 900g loaf tin.

175g butter
175g caster sugar
3 eggs
175g self raising flour
3 lemons, juice of 3 and
finely grated zest of 2

Cream butter and sugar. Add in the eggs, one at a time then fold in the flour along with the grated lemon zest from 2 of the lemons. Spoon the batter into the tin and bake for about 40 minutes or until cooked.

Remove the cake from the oven and prick the top of the cake using a fork.

50g caster sugar, extra

Stir 30g of the sugar into the juice of the 3 lemons and stir to dissolve sugar. Pour the mixture over the cake and sprinkle the last 20g of sugar over the cake. Leave to cool in the tin.

MADEIRA
CAKE

Madeira Cake

Cuts into 10 slices

Preheat oven to 160°C.

Butter and flour a 900g loaf tin.

200g butter, softened
200g caster sugar
4 eggs
200g self raising flour

Cream the butter until light and fluffy. Add the sugar and beat into the butter. Beat in the eggs one by one. Sieve the flour over the mixture and gently fold into the batter.

Pour into the cake tin and bake for approximately 40 minutes or until cooked through.

QUICK
SCONES

Quick Scones

Makes about 16

525g self raising flour
250ml milk
250ml cream

Preheat oven to 170°C.

Sift flour into a bowl. Shake milk and cream together then add to the flour. Mix to a firm dough and roll out onto a floured surface. Cut with a 5 or 6cm cutter and bake for 10-12 minutes.

BISCUITS AND SLICES

Simply 3 - 5

Biscuits and Slices

AMARETTI BISCUITS

Amaretti Biscuits

Makes 20

125g ground almonds
220g caster sugar
2 large egg whites
½ tsp vanilla essence
2 drops almond essence

Preheat oven to 160°C.

Beat almonds, sugar, egg whites and essences with electric whisk, on medium speed for 3 minutes then leave to stand for 5 minutes.

Spoon mixture into piping bag fitted with 1cm plain tube; pipe in circular motion from centre to make biscuits about 4cm in diameter leaving 2cm in between each.

Bake for about 12 minutes or until tops are browned lightly. Leave on trays for 5 minutes before putting on cooling rack.

Note: Can be made 3 days ahead and stored in an airtight container.
These biscuits can be used for the White Chocolate Torte in the Desserts Section.

CLASSIC OAT FLAPJACKS

Classic Oat Flapjacks

Makes 12

175g butter, cut into pieces
140g golden syrup
50g light muscovado sugar
250g porridge oats

Preheat the oven to 160°C.

Line the base of a shallow 23cm square tin with baking paper.

Put the butter, syrup and sugar in a saucepan and stir over a low heat until the butter has melted and the sugar has dissolved. Remove from the heat and stir in the oats.

Press the mixture into the tin. Bake for 20-25 minutes until golden brown on top.

Allow to cool in the tin for 5 minutes then mark into bars or squares with the back of a knife. Cool in the tin completely before cutting right through and removing.

Note: We think this is the best flapjack recipe we have tasted to date.

COCONUT MACAROONS

Coconut Macaroons

Makes 12

2 egg whites
100g caster sugar
160g desiccated coconut

Preheat oven to 170°C.

Whisk the egg whites, sugar and coconut together in a bowl until they lightly come together. With wet hands, press the mixture into a flat, square shape about 1cm high, on a board.

Cut out 12 x 5cm rounds, using a small pastry cutter and place on a lightly oiled baking tray.

Bake in the centre of the oven for about 15 minutes until very lightly golden. Transfer the macaroons to a wire tray to cool.

Note: These will keep in an airtight container for up to a week.

CORNFLAKE SLICE

Cornflake Slice

Makes 12 slices

Preheat oven to 180°C.

Lightly grease an 18 x 28cm tin. Line the base and sides with greased foil extending the foil 5cm over the long sides.

200g dark chocolate, melted

Spread the melted chocolate evenly over the base of the tin and chill for 5 minutes or until set.

110g sultanas
100g cornflakes, crushed
75g unsalted peanuts
170ml condensed milk

Combine the sultanas, cornflakes, peanuts and condensed milk in a bowl. Spread the mixture evenly over the chocolate base using the back of a spoon to level it.

Bake in the oven for 15 minutes or until set. Cool, then refrigerate until firm.

Cut into squares to serve.

DOUBLE CHOCOLATE SLICE

Double Chocolate Slice

Makes 24 slices

250g dark chocolate, melted

150g dark chocolate, roughly chopped
135g walnuts, roughly chopped
165g brown sugar
3 eggs

Preheat oven to 180°C.

Lightly grease an 18 x 28cm shallow tin. Line the base and sides with foil extending the foil 5cm over the long sides.

Spread the melted chocolate over the base of the pan and chill for 5 minutes or until set.

Place the chopped chocolate, walnuts, sugar and eggs in a food processor and process until combined. Pour the mixture over the chocolate base.

Bake for 20 minutes or until firm. Allow to cool. Turn out the slice and carefully remove the foil.

Cut slice into squares to serve.

JAM BISCUITS

Simply 3 - 5

Jam Biscuits

Makes 30

200g self raising flour
100g caster sugar
100g soft butter
1 small egg, beaten

15 tsp jam, approx

Preheat oven to 170°C.

Use a food processor to mix flour, sugar and butter together. Add just enough egg to form a stiff dough.

Roll into walnut sized balls and place on a baking tray. Flatten each ball slightly and make an indentation with your thumb. Drop ½ tsp of jam in centre. Bake 10-15 minutes until just golden. Cool on wire rack.

Note: Use any flavour jam you like or even use a couple of different flavoured jams.

MUESLI SLICE

Muesli Slice

Makes about 16 pieces

Preheat oven to 180°C.

Brush a 20 x 30cm tin with melted butter. Line the base and two opposite long sides with baking paper, allowing it to overhang a little.

580g toasted muesli
1 x 395ml can condensed milk
190g dark chocolate bits
50g almond flakes

Combine the muesli, condensed milk, chocolate bits and almonds in a large bowl.

Spoon into the prepared tin and smooth the surface. Bake for 30 minutes or until golden brown and set. Set aside for 30 minutes to cool.

Cut into rectangles to serve.

PEANUT BUTTER COOKIES

Simply 3 - 5

Peanut Butter Cookies

Makes 30

260g peanut butter, crunchy or smooth
220g caster sugar
1 egg, lightly beaten

Preheat oven to 180°C.

Combine all ingredients in a bowl and stir until combined.

Roll rounded teaspoons of the mixture into balls. Place about 5cms apart on greased baking sheets and flatten slightly with a fork. Bake in the oven for 15 minutes or until golden brown. Stand for 5 minutes then cool on a wire rack.

Note: These biscuits freeze well.

PECAN BISCUITS

Simply 3 - 5

Pecan Biscuits

Makes 24 small biscuits

90g pecan halves
50g butter
4 tbsp icing sugar, plus extra for
dusting
1 tsp vanilla essence
120g plain flour

Preheat oven to 180°C.

Lightly grease 2 oven trays.

Set aside 24 pecan halves to put on the top of biscuits and finely chop the remaining nuts. Cream the butter, icing sugar and vanilla together until light and fluffy. Add the chopped nuts and stir in the sifted flour in two batches. Using floured hands roll teaspoonfuls of the mixture into balls and place 2.5cm apart on the trays.

Press half a pecan nut onto each ball, flattening each slightly. Bake for 8-10 minutes or until light golden brown. Cool on trays and dust with icing sugar to serve.

Note: These are bite sized biscuits which are lovely to serve with coffee.

ROCKY ROAD SLICE

Rocky Road Slice

Makes 24 pieces

400g dark chocolate, chopped

250g marshmallows, halved
140g unsalted roasted peanuts
100g glace cherries, halved

Line the base of an 18 x 28cm shallow tin with foil or baking paper.

Melt the chocolate in a bowl over a saucepan of gently simmering water and spread one quarter over the base of the tin (you don't need to smooth it out).

Sprinkle the marshmallows, nuts and cherries over the chocolate and press them in lightly so that they stick.

Pour the remaining chocolate over the ingredients in the tin as evenly as you can. Tap the tin to make sure the chocolate gets into all the gaps.

Place the tin in the fridge for 20 minutes or until the chocolate is completely set. Lift out of the tin and remove the paper or foil and slice.

Note: Use a really sharp knife to get a clean cut.

SIMPLE
SHORTBREAD

Simple Shortbread

Makes 25 large or 40 small

250g butter
250g plain flour
125g self raising flour
125g caster sugar, plus extra for
dipping

Preheat oven to 150°C.

Process all ingredients together in a food processor. Place on a lightly floured surface and gently knead until smooth. Cut into shapes and bake for 20 minutes or until light golden and firm to touch.

When cool dip in extra caster sugar.

SMARTIE COOKIES

Smartie Cookies

Makes 14

100g butter, softened,
plus extra for greasing
100g light muscovado sugar
1 tbsp golden syrup

150g self raising flour
85g Smarties (about 3 tubes)

Preheat oven to 160°C.

Beat the butter and sugar together in a bowl until light and creamy then beat in the syrup.

Work in half the flour. Stir in the Smarties with the remaining half of flour and work the dough together with your fingers. Divide into 14 balls.

Place them well apart on baking sheets to allow for spreading. Don't flatten them.

Bake for about 12 minutes or until pale golden at the edges. Cool on a wire rack.

Note: Delicious. We save a few smarties to press onto the biscuits when they come out of the oven while they are still soft.

DRINKS

Simply 3 - 5

Drinks

Banana Milkshake   419
Serves 6

Champagne Punch   419
Serves 20

Ginger and Lemon Tea   419
Serves 2

Ginger Beer   421
Serves 6-8

Iced Lime Refresher   421
Makes about 5 Glasses

Limoncello   423
Makes 850ml

Orange and Cardamom Tea   425
Serves 2

Orange Hot Chocolate   425
Serves 2-3

Raspberry Smoothie   425
Makes 2 large smoothies

BANANA MILKSHAKE

CHAMPAGNE PUNCH

GINGER AND LEMON TEA

Simply 3 - 5

Banana Milkshake

Serves 6

1 litre semi skimmed milk, cold
2 ripe bananas, chopped

6 scoops vanilla ice cream

Put milk and bananas into a blender and blend until frothy.

Serve in tall glasses with a scoop of ice cream.

Champagne Punch

Serves 20

1.5 litres tropical fruit juice
2 x 750ml bottles champagne or sparkling wine
250g strawberries, quartered
2 oranges, sliced
ice cubes

Pour the juice and champagne into a large bowl. Add the strawberries and orange slices and stir together. Add ice cubes as required.

Ginger and Lemon Tea

Serves 2

6 slices peeled ginger
6 slices of lemon
1 tsp honey
600ml boiling water

Put all these ingredients together and leave to infuse for 5 minutes. Strain and serve with an extra slice of lemon if you wish.

GINGER BEER

ICED LIME REFRESHER

Ginger Beer

Serves 6-8

150g fresh ginger, peeled

Finely grate the ginger. Place in a bowl and pour over 750ml of boiling water. Stand for 2 hours.

125ml lemon juice
220g caster sugar
1 litre chilled water, approximately

Strain the ginger liquid and add the lemon juice and sugar. Stand for 30 minutes or until the sugar has dissolved. Add the chilled water to taste just before serving.

Note: The ginger beer will separate so just stir it before serving. You can add chilled fizzy water if you prefer.

Iced Lime Refresher

Makes about 5 glasses

1 litre water
150g caster sugar
80ml lime juice
1 tsp shredded mint leaves

Combine water, sugar, juice and mint in a large bowl and stir until sugar is dissolved. Cover and refrigerate for 4 hours or until well chilled.

ice cubes

Strain into jug and serve poured over ice cubes.

Note: This drink is served in India with spicy foods. Also good with a drop of gin or vodka!

LIMONCELLO

Simply 3 - 5

Limoncello

Makes 850ml

5 unwaxed lemons

Using a zester, very finely zest the lemon peel (or use a potato peeler and then cut the strips into fine shreds), making sure you don't use any of the white bitter pith.

150g caster sugar
500ml vodka or gin

Squeeze the juice from the lemons then make up to 500ml with water, place in a pan with the sugar and bring to the boil. Boil for 10 minutes until reduced by about a third then allow to cool. When cool, mix with the vodka and lemon zest.

Place in a large clean, sterilised bottle with either a screw cap or a cork. Store in a dark cupboard for 7-10 days, shaking the contents every day. If preferred, strain the liqueur to remove the peel and the sediment so that the liqueur is clear, though this isn't essential.

This will keep for a month, or can be kept frozen for longer. The alcohol will stop the liqueur freezing and it is delicious served straight from the freezer.

Note: We don't strain the lemon peel out of the liqueur, but that is because it is used very quickly! If you want to keep it for any length of time it would be best to strain it.

ORANGE AND CARDAMOM TEA

ORANGE HOT CHOCOLATE

RASPBERRY SMOOTHIE

Simply 3 - 5

Orange and Cardamom Tea

Serves 2

8 slices of orange
4 cardamom seeds, crushed lightly
2 tsp clear honey
600ml boiling water

Infuse all these ingredients together for 5 minutes. Strain and serve with an extra slice of orange if you wish.

Orange Hot Chocolate

Serves 2-3

500ml milk
2 strips orange peel
100g dark chocolate, chopped

Put milk, orange peel and chocolate into a pan and stir over a low heat until the chocolate has melted.

Strain mixture into a jug and pour into heatproof glasses.

Note: You can top this drink with whipped cream, orange zest and chocolate shavings if you wish.

Raspberry Smoothie

Makes 2 large smoothies

375ml milk
150g frozen raspberries
2 scoops vanilla ice cream
3 tbsp strawberry yoghurt
1 tbsp honey

Place all ingredients into a food processor or blender. Process until smooth and serve immediately.

EXTRAS

Simply 3 - 5

Extras

CHEAT'S FLAKY PASTRY

Simply 3 - 5

Cheat's Flaky Pastry

Note: Put the butter wrapped in foil in freezer for 30 minutes.

175g plain flour

Sift flour into bowl.

110g butter

Remove the butter from the freezer and coarsely grate into the bowl of flour.

With a knife mix the butter into the flour trying to coat all the butter with flour.

about 2 tbsp cold water
a drop of lemon juice

Add the cold water and a drop of lemon juice and continue to mix with a knife until the pastry comes together. Use your hands to finish it off, adding a little more water if needed.

Chill for 30 minutes before using.

CHOCOLATE ICING

CUCUMBER PICKLE

Chocolate Icing

Enough for 20cm cake

200g dark chocolate
50g butter
2 tsp golden syrup

Melt the chocolate in a bowl set over a pan of gently simmering water. When melted stir in the butter and golden syrup. Remove from the heat and leave to cool until spreadable.

Note: This goes well with the Chocolate Cake in the Cakes and Scones Section.

Cucumber Pickle

Makes about 3 x 450g jars

900g unpeeled cucumber, thinly sliced
350g sugar
1 tbsp salt
225ml cider vinegar or white wine vinegar

Put the cucumber in a large bowl, add the sugar, salt and vinegar, and mix well to combine.

Note: This pickle is great with cold meats, cheese, burgers and fish. It will keep for weeks although it will lose its colour.

LEMON AND GARLIC CROUTONS

Simply 3 - 5

Lemon and Garlic Croutons

Enough for 6

Preheat oven to 180°C.

Lightly grease an oven tray.

2 cloves garlic, peeled
40ml lemon juice

Blend the garlic and lemon juice with 3 tbsp water in a small blender until smooth.

150g ciabatta, chopped into small cubes

Toss the bread in the mixture and mix evenly. Place on the oven tray and bake for 15 minutes or until crunchy.

Note: If you don't want to put the oven on just for these they can be cooked under the grill. They are great served on top of soup or scattered over salads.

MIXED BERRY JAM

ORANGE ICING

Mixed Berry Jam

Makes about 4 x 450g jars

1kg mixed summer berries
600ml apple juice

Put the fruit and apple juice in a preserving pan or large saucepan and bring to a gentle simmer. Simmer for about 5 minutes stirring a couple of times.

1kg sugar

Add the sugar and stir until it dissolves. Increase the heat and bring to a hard boil. Boil for 10-15 minutes, remove from heat and test for setting. To test put a teaspoonful of jam onto a very cold saucer and push the jam with your finger. It will wrinkle if it is ready.

Boil for a little longer if not quite set.

Leave for 15 minutes, stir to distribute fruit and put in warm sterilised jars.

Note: Frozen berries can be used to make this jam.

Orange Icing

Enough to top a 900g loaf cake

120g icing sugar
40g butter, softened
2 tbsp orange juice
½ tsp finely grated orange zest

Sift the icing sugar into a bowl and add all the other ingredients. Mix until smooth.

Note: This goes well with the Orange Cake in the Cakes and Scones Section.

PIZZA DOUGH

Pizza Dough

Makes 4 x 23cm bases

700g strong white bread flour
2 tsp salt
1 tsp sugar
1 sachet easy blend dried yeast

450ml warm water

Sift the flour, salt, sugar and yeast into a large bowl.

Add water and mix to a dough in the bowl and then put on floured work surface. Knead for 10 minutes until smooth and elastic. Shape into a ball and put in a lightly oiled bowl, cover with cling film. Leave in a warm place for about 1 hour or until doubled in size.

Knead the dough again until smooth then divide into 4 pieces. Roll each piece into a 23cm round and place on greased baking trays. Leave for 20 minutes to rise again.

Preheat oven to 220°C. Brush the pizza bases with oil and cover with toppings of your choice. Bake for 15-20 minutes until lightly browned.

PRALINE TRUFFLES

Praline Truffles

Makes about 40

Praline

100g caster sugar
100g almonds, skin on

Put a sheet of baking paper on a baking tray. Place sugar and almonds in a non stick frying pan over medium heat. Allow sugar to caramelise slowly (do not stir just swirl pan). Cook until sugar has caramelised to a rich golden brown. Pour onto paper and allow to cool completely.

When cool process in a food processor or place in a bag and bash with a rolling pin until you have the texture of breadcrumbs. Any leftover praline can be used to sprinkle over ice cream.

Truffles

150ml single cream
250g dark chocolate, chopped
1 tbsp brandy (optional)

Place cream in saucepan and bring to boil. Add chocolate and brandy. Stir until chocolate has melted and mixture is smooth. Pour into a shallow dish and put in fridge for about 30 minutes until set. Roll into balls and drop into a bowl of praline turning to cover.

Note: The praline will keep for up to a month in an airtight jar. Pop the finished truffles into little petit four cases and serve with coffee.

QUICK
SAVOURY
PASTRY

Quick Savoury Pastry

225g plain flour
100g butter, cubed

Place flour and butter in food processor, and process in short bursts until the mixture resembles breadcrumbs.

3-4 tbsp cold water

Add water and process for a further 20-30 seconds only until the mixture starts to form a ball around the blades. Turn out onto a floured work surface, knead gently until smooth. Wrap in clingfilm and chill for at least 30 minutes.

Variations:

Cheese pastry – Add 1 teaspoon of English mustard powder to the flour. Stir in 100g of finely grated mature Cheddar cheese, to the mixture at the breadcrumb stage. Ideal for cheese straws and vegetable pies.

Herb pastry – Add 3 tablespoons of freshly chopped herbs, such as parsley, thyme, chives, oregano or basil with the flour. Great for quiches and chicken pies.

Olive pastry – Add 50g finely chopped green or black olives, to the mixture at the breadcrumb stage. Delicious with a tomato and mozzarella filling.

QUICK SWEET PASTRY

Quick Sweet Pastry

225g plain flour
50g caster sugar
150g unsalted butter, cubed

Place flour, sugar and butter in food processor. Process in short bursts until the mixture resembles breadcrumbs.

1 medium egg yolk
2-3 tbsp cold water

Add egg yolk and water to processor and process for a further 20-30 seconds until the mixture starts to form a ball around the blades. Turn out onto a floured work surface and knead gently until smooth. Wrap in clingfilm and chill for at least 30 minutes.

Variations:

Almond pastry – replace 75g flour with ground almonds

Cinnamon pastry – add 1 teaspoon of ground cinnamon to the flour.

ROSEMARY AND GARLIC OIL

TOMATO CHUTNEY

Simply 3 - 5

Rosemary and Garlic Oil

Use a large bottle with a tight fitting lid.

10 cloves garlic, peeled and finely sliced
1 bunch rosemary
600ml olive oil

Insert the garlic and rosemary into the bottle. Pour the olive oil into the bottle ensuring the garlic and rosemary are covered with the oil.

Close and leave to stand for 3 weeks before using, shaking the bottle from time to time. Strain and store in a cool, dark place.

Note: Use to brush meat, poultry or vegetables prior to cooking. It is also great for roasting potatoes.

Tomato Chutney

1 x 400g can chopped tomatoes
1 red onion, finely chopped
4 tbsp red wine vinegar
2 tbsp brown sugar
2 tbsp sweet chilli sauce

Place all the ingredients into a saucepan. Simmer for 30 minutes, stirring occasionally.

445

YORKSHIRE PUDDINGS

Simply 3 - 5

Yorkshire Puddings

Serves 4

60g plain flour
2 eggs, beaten
100ml milk

2 tbsp sunflower oil

Preheat oven to 200°C.

Sift the flour into a bowl. Make a well in the centre then pour in the beaten eggs and gradually mix in the flour. Quickly add the milk and, using a hand whisk, whisk until you have a smooth batter.

Place the oil in a 12 hole patty tin and heat on the top shelf of the oven for about 5 minutes. Stir the batter and transfer to a jug then pour into the tins so that it comes about halfway up the sides.

Bake for 15-20 minutes until crisp and golden brown.

INDEX OF RECIPES

Simply 3 - 5
Index of Recipes

Simply 3 - 5
Index of Recipes

Simply 3 - 5
Index of Recipes

Simply 3 - 5
Index of Recipes

GLOSSARY
OF
INGREDIENTS

Simply 3 - 5
Glossary of Ingredients

Almond essence
A synthetically produced essence used sparingly to impart an almond flavour to foods

Antipasto chargrilled vegetables
A combination of chargrilled vegetables often consisting of red pepper, aubergine, courgette etc

Arrabiatta pasta sauce
A tomato pasta sauce with peppers and chilli

Baking powder
A raising agent consisting of two parts cream of tartar to one part bicarbonate of soda (baking soda) used for batters, cakes and pastry

Balsamic vinegar
Balsamic vinegar is a fragrant vinegar, dark in colour, offering a sweet, mellow flavour

Barbecue sauce
A spicy, tomato based, brown coloured sauce

Basil
A popular herb with a sweet peppery flavour which suits tomato, chicken and shellfish and can also be added to pastas, stir fries, salads and soups

Basil Pesto
A sauce made from basil, garlic, olive oil, pine nuts and Parmesan cheese

Basmati rice
A long grained rice that has a distinctive fragrance and a delicate flavour

Black bean sauce
A Chinese sauce made from fermented soy beans, spices, water and wheat flour

Black olive tapenade
A spread consisting of black olives, capers, anchovies, seasonings, and olive oil

Black treacle
A thick syrup with a distinctively strong flavour, slightly bitter with a rich colour

Blue vein cheese
A mould treated cheese mottled with blue veining. Varieties include firm and crumbly Stilton types to mild, creamy Brie like cheeses

Bouquet Garni
A bunch of herbs, usually parsley, thyme and bay leaves tied with string and used to flavour stock, soups and stews. The bouquet garni is usually removed before serving

Brie
A soft creamy white cheese which when ripe (ready to eat or 'ready to go') has a 'runny' texture with a flavour that has become stronger with age

Cajun seasoning
Has a very spicy flavour and is a blend of assorted herbs and spices which can include paprika, basil, onion, fennel, thyme, cayenne and tarragon

Camembert
A soft, rich, creamy partly ripened cheese

Cannellini beans
Small kidney shaped white beans, mild in flavour

Simply 3 - 5
Glossary of Ingredients

Capers
Capers have a salty, sour flavour and are added to a range of dishes to add piquancy and a unique taste. Are available either dried and salted or pickled in vinegar

Cardamom seeds
Have an aromatic spicy sweet flavour and are traditionally used in Indian food

Cava
A Spanish sparkling wine made by the champagne method

Cayenne pepper
A spice made from small dried chillies, spicy with a pungent flavour

Chestnut mushrooms
Similar in appearance to the button mushroom, but darker in colour with a stronger flavour

Chickpeas
These medium sized legumes have a sweet nutty flavour, retain their shape during cooking and are great in couscous dishes, salads, stews and curries

Chives
A relative of the onion and garlic, chives have a mild subtle onion flavour

Chorizo sausage
A firm, spicy pork sausage highly seasoned with garlic and chillies

Ciabatta
A long, flattish, crusty, Italian yeast bread loaf, made with white flour and olive oil

Cider vinegar
This is a smooth, refined vinegar with low acidity made from unprocessed apple cider and it often has a distinct apple flavour

Cinnamon
Usually sold in rolled up sticks (quills) or ground powder and has a sweet, distinctive flavour and aroma

Coconut cream
Coconut cream is very similar to coconut milk but contains less water. The difference is mainly consistency. It has a thicker, more paste like consistency, while coconut milk is generally a liquid

Coconut milk
Coconut milk is a sweet milk derived from the meat of the coconut. Available in cans and cartons at supermarkets

Condensed milk
A canned milk product consisting of milk with more than half the water content removed and sugar added to the milk that remains

Coriander
A bright green leafed herb with a mild sweet citrus like flavour. Also available as seeds or ground

Couscous
A fine, grain like mild flavoured cereal made from semolina

Cream cheese
A soft cow's milk cheese which is mild and velvety

Crème fraiche
A cultured thick cream, with a fresh sour taste. If unavailable substitute with sour cream

Cumin
A spice that has a powerful, earthy, nutty flavour and aroma and is available whole or ground

Demerara sugar
A coarse, light brown sugar

Desiccated coconut
Finely shredded natural unsweetened, dried coconut flesh

Dijon mustard
French mustard with a smooth creamy consistency and a mild flavour it is made with brown mustard seeds, salt, spices and verjuice

Simply 3 - 5
Glossary of Ingredients

Dill
A herb with fine feathery leaves which have a parsley like sweet, aromatic flavor with overtones of anise

Double cream
Has a 48 per cent fat content and is particularly good for whipping as well using in sauces as it can be boiled for reduction

Dry vermouth
Dry vermouth is a fortified wine flavoured with aromatic herbs and spices

English mustard
English mustard is typically bright yellow in appearance and very hot in flavour

Feta cheese
A crumbly milk cheese with a sharp salty taste

Five spice powder
A classic fragrant Asian spice mixture of ground cinnamon, cloves, star anise, Sichuan and fennel seeds

Flat leaf parsley
Also known as continental or Italian parsley it is sweeter than the standard curly leaf variety, and at the same time more flavourful

French mustard
French mustard is a dark coloured mustard containing more vinegar than some mustards and therefore has a milder taste

Fromage frais
Fromage frais is a fresh, soft curd cheese that is low in fat. It has a slightly tangy taste

Garam masala
A blend of ground spices, including cardamom, cinnamon, cumin, cloves, coriander and fennel, which is often used in Indian cuisine

Gelatine leaves
Used as a setting agent

Ginger
A gnarled bumpy root bulb with a peppery slightly sweet flavour with notes of lemon and rosemary and a spicy, pungent aroma. Also sold in a ground form

Glace cherries
Cherries cooked in a heavy sugar syrup then dried

Goat cheese
Made from goat milk, goat cheese is a soft white cheese which has an earthy, strong taste

Golden syrup
A sweet, thick liquid obtained in the process of manufacturing cane sugar or glucose

Gorgonzola cheese
A veined Italian blue cheese made from unskimmed cow's milk and/or goat's milk. It can be buttery or firm with a salty, strong flavour. The name comes from Gorgonzola, a small town near Milan

Green curry paste
The hottest of the traditional curry pastes. Particularly good in chicken and vegetable curries, a great addition to stir fries and noodle dishes

Gruyere cheese
A hard, yellow cheese made from cow's milk, named after the town of Gruyeres in Switzerland. It has a sweet and slightly salty flavour

457

Simply 3 - 5
Glossary of Ingredients

Halloumi
A firm cream coloured milk cheese matured in brine and salty in flavour. Can be served fresh or grilled / fried, briefly, without breaking down

Hoisin sauce
A thick, sweet and spicy sauce made from soy beans garlic and spices, popular within Asian cuisine

Hollandaise sauce
A classic base sauce of butter and lemon juice thickened with egg yolks over gentle heat

Horseradish sauce
A sauce made from grated horseradish root, vinegar and cream

Jalapenos
A moderately hot, green short tapering chilli with thick flesh which is available fresh, canned or in jars

Jarlsberg cheese
A mild Swiss style cheese which has large irregular holes. The texture is buttery rich and the flavour mild and slightly sweet

Kalamata olives
Brine cured black olives usually packed in olive oil or vinegar and split to better absorb the marinade

Madras curry paste
Madras curry paste is a Southern Indian hot curry paste which includes cumin, coriander and chilli

Mint
A highly flavoured herb with textured, bright green leaves with spearmint and peppermint being the most common

Mozzarella cheese
A semi soft cheese with a delicate flavour and a stringy texture when heated. Mozzarella is suitable for dishes that require melted cheese

Muscovado sugar
Muscovado is a type of unrefined brown sugar which has a strong molasses flavour, also available in a lighter milder flavour

Nutmeg
The dried nut of an evergreen tree the nutmeg has an oval shape and smooth texture with a strong, sweet aroma and flavour

Oregano
An aromatic, spicy Mediterranean herb with a pungent, peppery flavour sold as fresh sprigs or chopped dried leaves

Pancetta
An Italian style salt cured but not smoked rolled pork belly available in slices

Paprika
A spice made from ground dried peppers available sweet or hot

Parma ham
A raw, pressed ham that has been spiced during the curing process

Parmesan cheese
A sharp strong tasting hard cheese also known as Parmigiano

Parsley
Parsley is one of the most popular herbs used in cooking. Curly leaf parsley is best known for garnishing and has a milder flavour than flat leaf or Italian parsley which is often used in a bouquet garni. Flat leaf parsley both has a stronger flavour and holds up to longer cooking

Passatta
Passatta is a thick rich, pulpy tomato puree usually available in bottles from supermarkets

Pesto sauce
An Italian sauce traditionally made from basil, garlic, olive oil, pine nuts and Parmesan cheese, however different flavours are increasingly being developed

Simply 3 - 5
Glossary of Ingredients

Pine nuts
Pine nuts are small, cream coloured kernels from the cones of pine trees and have a very delicate flavour

Pith
The spongy, fibrous white lining the rind and surrounding the sections of citrus fruits

Pitta bread
Also known as lebanese bread this wheat flour pocket bread is sold in small or large flat pieces that separate easily into two thin rounds

Plum tomatoes
Plum tomatoes are oval or cylindrical in shape, with significantly fewer seed compartments than standard round tomatoes and a generally higher solid content which makes them very suitable for processing/pureeing

Portobello mushrooms
Large brown mushrooms with a deep musty smell and a meaty texture that gets better the longer the mushrooms are cooked

Prosciutto
An unsmoked Italian ham which has been salted and air dried, usually sold thinly sliced

Ras El Hanout
A traditional blend of Moroccan spices used in many North African dishes. It can include paprika, cumin, ginger, orris root, saffron, dried flowers, ginger, turmeric, fennel and bay leaf

Red curry paste
Red curry paste is milder than green curry paste and is used in soups, curries and stir fries

Red lentils
Red lentils are a legume and tend to disintegrate with long cooking because the hulls have been removed. Slightly sweet in flavour, these work well for soup

Red mild chillies
Red chillies are hot peppers which have varying degrees of spiciness but generally, the smaller the chilli the hotter it will be. Always wash hands thoroughly after preparing chillies and avoid contact with eyes and other sensitive tissue

Red wine vinegar
A vinegar obtained from fermented red wine which has a tangy complex, mellow flavour

Redcurrant jelly
A preserve made from redcurrants, used as a glaze for desserts and meats or in sauces

Rice wine vinegar
A mild white vinegar good for salads and used in Chinese cuisine

Ricotta cheese
A fresh creamy soft, sweet, moist white cheese with a slightly grainy texture. Made from whey, a by product of other cheese making, to which fresh milk and acid are added

Risotto rice
A plump white rice that can absorb lots of liquid without going mushy. It is considered that Italy produces the best

Rocket
A dark green leaf with a strong, spicy, peppery flavour. Baby rocket is smaller and less peppery

Simply 3 - 5
Glossary of Ingredients

Rolled oats
Whole oat grains that have been steamed and flattened

Roquefort
A strong cheese with a bluish mould, made from goats' and ewes' milk

Rosemary
A strong, aromatic herb, used to season meat, poultry, and vegetables. Sold as fresh sprigs or dried leaves

Sage
A grey green leaf herb with a slightly bitter flavour and distinctive aroma. Sold as fresh sprigs or dried leaves

Salsa
A combination of tomato, onion, pepper, vinegar, herbs and spices available in a chunky style and varying degrees of spiciness

Satay sauce
A popular Indonesian/Malaysian spicy peanut sauce

Semidried tomatoes
Semidried tomatoes are sweeter and softer than sundried tomatoes. They are moist and plump and purchased in oil

Semi skimmed milk
Milk which has a lower fat content than regular milk

Sesame oil
Made from roasted, crushed white sesame seeds and not generally used for frying. Is used to add flavour to dishes

Sesame seeds
Crispy little seeds with a mild flavour. When toasted sesame seeds acquire a nuttier taste. Sesame seeds may be used in savoury dishes or desserts, and are often sprinkled on baked foods

Shallots
Also known as eschalots or French shallots. Small, golden brown or red onion bulbs, grown in clusters

Single cream
Has an 18 per cent fat content and is a good pouring or coffee cream. It needs to be cooked at lower temperatures than double cream and must not be boiled

Sour cream
A cream, only mildly sour in taste, soured and thickened either naturally or artificially and can be used for cooking, dressings and dips

Soy sauce
Made from fermented soy beans. Several variations are available including salt reduced, light and sweet. Light soy sauce is generally saltier than dark soy sauce

Sponge finger biscuits
Sweet and light finger shaped biscuits made from sponge cake mixture, also known as savoiardi

Spring onions
Immature onions which have a white base that has not fully developed into a bulb and green leaves that are long and straight. Both parts are edible

Stilton cheese
A rich strong smelling and tasting crumbly cheese with veins of blue green mould

Sundried tomatoes/paste
Tomatoes which traditionally were dried by the sun, but now often in ovens. Have an intense tomato flavor and are often made in to a paste

Sweet chilli sauce
Sweet chilli sauce is a Thai type sauce made from red chillies, sugar, garlic and white wine vinegar

Simply 3 - 5
Glossary of Ingredients

Tabasco sauce
A hot spicy chilli pepper sauce which needs to be used sparingly

Tandoori paste
Tandoori curry paste is a tasty and flavoursome blend of tamarind, coriander, garlic, ginger and various other spices

Tarragon
A fragrant, distinctively sweet herb sold as fresh sprigs or dried chopped

Tartare sauce
A mayonnaise with added pickles and sometimes capers, shallots and parsley which is served as an accompaniment to seafood

Tempura batter
A light batter, common in Japanese cuisine, and used to coat delicately flavoured foods before frying

Teriyaki marinade
A homemade or commercially bottled sauce usually made from soy sauce, mirin, sugar, ginger and other spices

Thyme
The leaves have a strong, slightly lemony flavour and aroma and can be used fresh or dried

Tikka paste
Tikka curry paste is a mild paste which has an aromatic, slightly smoky, rich flavour

Tomato ketchup
See Tomato sauce

Tomato paste
Very concentrated tomato puree

Tomato puree
Is a sauce made from strained cooked tomatoes

Tomato sauce
A flavoured condiment made from slow cooked tomatoes, vinegar and spices

Tortilla wraps
Thin, round unleavened bread originating in Mexico. Available in wheat flour or corn varieties

Turmeric
A rich yellow powder which is intensely pungent in taste but not hot

Vanilla essence
An inexpensive substitute for pure vanilla extract, made with synthetic vanillin and other flavourings

Vanilla extract
A concentrated essence that has been made from the vanilla bean reduced in a sugar syrup

Wasabi / paste
Japanese horseradish which has a sharp hot flavour, most commonly found in a green paste form

White wine vinegar
White wine vinegar is a moderately tangy vinegar which has a hint of flavour of what the wine tasted like before it became vinegar

Wholegrain mustard
Also known as seeded mustard, it is made from crushed mustard seeds

Wild rice
The grains are long, slender and black, with a distinctive earthy, nutty flavour

Worcestershire sauce
A thin, dark brown spicy sauce used as a seasoning and condiment. Made from vinegar, molasses, golden syrup, salt, tamarind, anchovies, spices, onion powder, garlic powder, lemon oil and water

Zest
Coloured outer layer of citrus fruit skin containing the fruit's oil

461

Simply 3 · 5

GLOSSARY OF PREPARATION AND COOKING TERMS

Simply 3 - 5
Glossary of Preparation and Cooking Terms

Allow to rest
To loosely cover cooked meats and place in a warm place. This allows the meat to relax and the juices become reabsorbed back into the meat and to maintain its moisture during carving

Bake
A dry heat method of cooking in an oven at a temperature between 140°C and 280°C

Barbecue
To cook food using a direct heat method, usually outside, using a charcoal / wood fire or barbecue

Baste
To spoon hot fat or liquid over food as it cooks

Beat
To use a large spoon, or a rotary or electric beater, to turn ingredients over and over rapidly to make the mixture smooth and light

Blend
To mix together two or more ingredients until they are no longer separate

Boil
To bring liquids to boiling point so that large bubbles form, then break on the surface

Browning meat
To cook meat in a frying pan with oil or butter until it turns brown in colour, often used to seal the surface and retain juices

Caramelised
Cooking sugar or other foods until browned which develops a full rich, intense flavour. Vegetables, meats and seafood are often enhanced by a gentle browning that caramelises natural sugars

Core
To remove the central seeded area inside fruit

Coulis
A purèe of fruit or vegetables used as a light sauce

Cream butter and sugar
To beat butter, gradually adding sugar until the mixture is fluffy and creamy

Crystallise
The forming of sugar crystals

Curdle
The separation of milk or egg mixtures into liquid and solids generally caused by overcooking or excessive heat

Dice
Cut into small cubes

Drain
Empty food into a colander or drainer to separate the liquid from the solids

Drizzle
Pouring a liquid/sauce over food in a slow, light trickle

Fold
To incorporate lighter ingredients into denser ingredients without deflating, to make a light mixture by carefully stirring vertically down through the mixture, continuing across the bottom of the bowl and ending with an upward and over movement

Simply 3 - 5
Glossary of Preparation and Cooking Terms

Fry
Frying is the cooking of food in oil or fat

Garnish
To add an interesting edible ingredient to a plate or food to make it look more attractive

Grease and flour
To coat or rub a cake pan with oil/fat and then dust the pan with flour

Grill
To cook using dry heat either under an open grill or on a grill plate

Hulled
To remove the hull or calyx, which is the green leafy top of the strawberry, which is generally removed before cooking or serving

Infuse
A process of steeping or soaking any substance in liquid

Julienne
Technique of cutting vegetables, fruit or citrus rinds into matchstick sized strips

Knead
Kneading is repeating the folding and compressing of a dough, with your hands, to develop the gluten and mix ingredients together

Marinate
To allow a sauce or flavouring mixture (marinade) to absorb into food to flavour or prepare it for cooking

Medium rare
When cooking red meat this term refers to meat that is sealed on the outside, red in the middle but warm all the way through

Poach
To cook in water or seasoned liquid in an open pan at simmering point with just enough liquid to cover the food

Preheat
To turn the oven on to a certain temperature before starting to cook so the oven is at the correct temperature when you need to put something in to bake

Process
Breaking down food in a food processor until it is the desired consistency which, for example, could be mashed, breadcrumb like or smooth

Rare
When cooking red meat, this term refers to meat that is sealed on the outside, but leaving the meat red and tender and barely warm on the inside

Reduce
To boil liquid until it thickens by process of evaporation

Roast
To oven cook food in an uncovered pan at a high heat that produces a well browned surface and seals in the juices

Sauté
To fry briskly using a small amount of fat in a shallow frying pan over moderately high heat. The food is turned or tossed for even browning

Score
Make shallow incisions into the surface of food. Used to allow faster cooking time, allow other ingredients to add flavour or to shape/decorate the food

Sear
To seal the surface of a food quickly at high heat which can add colour and flavour to meat, chicken or fish in addition to retaining the juices

Season
Adding salt, pepper or other seasonings which enhances the flavour of the food being prepared

Simply 3 - 5
Glossary of Preparation and Cooking Terms

Shallow fry
Frying with little fat or with only sufficient fat to half immerse food

Sift
Shake dry ingredients through a sieve or sifter to remove lumps and aerate

Simmer
Heat a liquid mixture on medium heat so that small bubbles break on the surface but the mixture does not come to a full boil

Skim
Remove any floating material that rises to the surface of a liquid

Stand
To leave in a position of rest

Steam
A moist heat cooking method where food is placed in a basket or rack over (not in) a boiling liquid in a covered pan and is cooked by direct contact from the steam

Stir fry
To cook even sized pieces of food in a little oil in a frying pan or wok over a high heat while stirring continuously

Strain
To pass foods through a strainer or fine mesh separating the solids and liquids

Whip
To beat ingredients together quickly with a spoon or mixer to increase volume and incorporate air, often used for cream or egg whites

Whisk
To use a wire or electric whisk with a rapid up and down circular movement to incorporate air into mixtures and make them light

Notes